Sixth Edition

HOW TO DEVELOP A PROFESSIONAL PORTFOLIO

A MANUAL FOR TEACHERS

Dorothy M. Campbell
Beverly J. Melenyzer
Diane H. Nettles
Richard M. Wyman, Jr.
California University of Pennsylvania

PEARSON

Boston   Columbus   Indianapolis   New York   San Francisco   Upper Saddle River
Amsterdam   Cape Town   Dubai   London   Madrid   Milan   Munich   Paris   Montréal   Toronto
Delhi   Mexico City   São Paulo   Sydney   Hong Kong   Seoul   Singapore   Taipei   Tokyo

Vice President and Editorial Director: Jeffery W. Johnston
Senior Acquisitions Editor: Meredith Fossel
Editorial Assistant: Krista Slavicek
Vice President, Director of Marketing: Margaret Waples
Senior Marketing Manager: Christopher Barry
Senior Managing Editor: Pamela D. Bennett
Production Manager: Susan EW Hannahs
Senior Cover Art Director: Jayne Conte
Cover Designer: Suzanne Behnke
Cover Art: Cvijun/Fotolia
Full-Service Project Management: Jogender Taneja, Aptara®, Inc.
Composition: Aptara®, Inc.
Text and Cover Printer/Bindery: Courier/Westford
Text Font: 10/12 ITC Garamond Std

Credits and acknowledgments for material borrowed from other sources and reproduced, with permission, in this text appear on the appropriate page within the text.

Every effort has been made to provide accurate and current Internet information in this text. However, the Internet and information posted on it are constantly changing, so it is inevitable that some of the Internet addresses listed in this will change.

Library of Congress Cataloging-in-Publication Data

Campbell, Dorothy M.
  How to develop a professional portfolio: a manual for teachers/Dorothy M. Campbell, Beverly J. Melenyzer, Diane H. Nettles, Richard M. Wyman, Jr., California University of Pennsylvania.—Sixth edition.
     pages cm
  ISBN-13: 978-0-13-310117-1
  ISBN-10: 0-13-310117-7
  1. Teachers—Rating of—Handbooks, manuals, etc. 2. Portfolios in education—Handbooks, manuals, etc.
3. Teachers—Employment—Handbooks, manuals, etc. I. Title.
  LB2838.H56 2014
  371.14'4—dc23

                                                                                            2012044281

10 9 8 7 6 5 4 3 2 1

ISBN 10:   0-13-310117-7
ISBN 13: 978-0-13-310117-1

The authors dedicate this edition in memory of Dr. Gary Kennedy—
friend, mentor, colleague, and teacher extraordinaire.

PREFACE

How to Develop a Professional Portfolio: A Manual for Teachers has been a leading source of information for teachers who need guidance in creating a portfolio that showcases their professional abilities. This text has provided thousands of preservice and inservice teachers with the tools they needed to provide to others an authentic, broad-based, and compelling method for evaluating that work. In seven concise chapters, this edition offers step-by-step procedures for portfolio development, using national teaching standards as the organizing system. The text offers an extensive list of pragmatic artifact possibilities so that teachers can see the range of documents that are applicable to presenting their professional growth. Guidelines for using the portfolio throughout one's teaching career are included in Chapter 6, which also includes interview questions and ways to use the portfolio in an interview. The final chapter is devoted to showing teachers how to pull it all together in an electronic portfolio. Whether you are a preservice teacher, new teacher, tenured teacher, or master teacher, this edition can help answer questions you may have about creating your professional portfolio.

NEW TO THIS EDITION

The major revision to this sixth edition is the use of the revised Interstate Teacher Assessment and Support Consortium (InTASC) core teaching standards, which were published in April 2011. These standards address teaching performances, critical dispositions, and essential knowledge that facilitate learner achievement, and they reflect a new emphasis on teachers' impact on student learning. We have revised the entire text to include these changes in light of our continued commitment to the use of standards for developing professional portfolios.

The 2011 InTASC standards are explained and then represented with scenarios of actual preservice and inservice teaching activities for students of all levels, preschool through high school. Each scenario is followed by a description of the corresponding document and sample rationale.

An additional structure for organizing portfolios has been added in this edition. Danielson's Framework for Teaching, a research-based framework grounded in the constructivist model of learning and teaching, divides twenty-two components across four domains of teaching responsibility: planning and preparation (Domain 1), classroom environment (Domain 2), instruction (Domain 3), and professional responsibilities (Domain 4).

Chapter 5 is an annotated, alphabetized list of possible artifacts that can be used in a portfolio. This edition includes five new artifact possibilities that address InTASC Standard 5, Application of Content.

One of the most popular features of this text is the "Portfolio at a Glance." Now revised to reflect the 2011 InTASC standards, this brochure is especially helpful for teachers engaged in job searching and appreciated by the school administrators who interview prospective teachers.

In recent years, electronic portfolios have become commonplace. In Chapter 7, new links to online portfolios will provide the reader with additional examples of model electronic portfolios.

In summary, the sixth edition offers these revisions:

- The entire text has been revised to reflect the 2011 InTASC standards.
- Danielson's Framework for Teaching (FFT) domains have been added to Chapter 3 to provide an additional structure for organizing the portfolio.
- In Chapter 4, all ten explanations of standards and teaching scenarios are newly revised to reflect the new 2011 InTASC standards.
- Five additional artifact possibilities have been added to Chapter 5 to address InTASC Standard Five, Application of Content.
- Chapter 7 includes updated links to online electronic portfolios.
- In Appendix B, a newly revised "Portfolio at a Glance" provides readers with a useful tool for use in a job search.

SPECIAL FEATURES OF THIS TEXT

Readers and reviewers of our text have told us that they appreciate our engaging and user-friendly writing style. They also like that the text, while concise, is packed with practical, useful information. Several features of this text have been especially valued by preservice and inservice teachers who have used it as a guide for portfolio development. These features include the following:

- In a user-friendly, conversational style, the text offers step-by-step procedures for portfolio development and tips on how to organize portfolios.
- The text uses clearly explained national teaching standards as an example of an organizing system for the portfolio.
- The 2011 InTASC standards are explained and then represented with scenarios of actual preservice and inservice teaching activities for students of all levels, preschool through high school. Each scenario is followed by a description of the corresponding artifact and sample rationale.
- Chapter 5, titled "Artifact Possibilities" is an annotated, alphabetized list of 65 possible artifacts that teachers can include in their portfolios.
- The "Try This" applications remain popular with users; this interactive feature presents specific activities to jumpstart portfolio development.
- Chapter 7 is dedicated to the development of an electronic portfolio, using a step-by-step approach.
- Appendix B contains directions for creating the "Portfolio at a Glance." This brochure is especially helpful for teachers engaged in job searches.
- Teachers preparing for job searches will also value the sample interview questions, with tips on how to use portfolios effectively in interviews and evaluations.

TIME TO START

The time to start your portfolio is now. To allow portfolio work to achieve its full potential, you will need to view it as an ongoing process that enables you to chart your growth, set new goals, and design new paths for your professional development. When you consider portfolio work as a culminating event, you will organize and justify documentation of what you have already done well. By starting now, you can make your portfolio as much an "improving tool" as a "proving tool." Let it reflect you as a growing, changing professional who is committed to continuous improvement.

ACKNOWLEDGMENTS

The authors would like to thank Cheryl Hill of Roosevelt University, whose thoughtful inquiries began this revision process, and Debra Clarke and Yvonne Weaver, of Waynesburg University, for sharing their pioneering work in aligning InTASC standards with the Danielson's Framework for Teaching.

CONTENTS

1

What You Need to Know about Portfolios

WHY PORTFOLIOS?

Katie Smith sat at the end of a large conference table, surrounded by interviewers, all of whom were administrators or veteran teachers in the school district to which she was applying. Each of them had in front of him or her a brochure, called "Portfolio at a Glance," which Katie had prepared and mailed to the district personnel office a week ago. On the first page of this brochure was the access information to her electronic portfolio. This brochure briefly summarized several of the documents in Katie's professional portfolio. Its purpose was to capture the highlights of her preservice experiences, as showcased in her portfolio. She used the brochure as a way of introducing herself and her portfolio to her prospective employers. Katie also had with her the notebook that contained the hard-copy contents of her portfolio.

One of the principals at the table began the interview. He said, "Ms. Smith, I see from your brochure that you have had some experience working in middle school. Tell us about this."

"Well," said Katie, "I completed the first half of my student teaching assignment in middle school, in which I taught seventh-grade social studies and language arts classes.

I had a wonderful experience because I was able to use so many of the strategies that I had learned in my methods courses at the university. My supervising teacher encouraged me to use constructivist strategies, along with cooperative learning. I'm so glad that I did because I found that seventh graders need to be actively involved in their learning, just as the younger children do. As you can see in my brochure, I outlined one of the lessons that I taught in the social studies class. During this lesson, the students researched and then reenacted the Boston Tea Party. One of the district goals is for them to retell important events in the Revolutionary War period, so I thought that role playing and drama would enhance their memory of dates and people. I have photographs of this lesson in the portfolio that I brought with me today. Here, I can find them for you."

Katie quickly turned to a page in her portfolio and put a bookmark on the page. She handed it to the principal.

"A video of this lesson is included in my electronic portfolio, which is on this disk," she continued. "You can access the file and view it at your leisure, if you wish."

The principal leaned back in his chair as he examined the document. "Hmm, interesting," he said. "I would like to see your electronic portfolio, too. But first, tell me, how did you manage the behavior of all those seventh graders while they completed this reenactment?"

Katie smiled. "I was a little nervous at first. But I knew that if my students saw a purpose for their learning and if they were able to make some of their own choices in the project, their interest would be high, and I'd have fewer problems with misbehavior. And it worked! In fact, my supervising teacher spoke highly of my classroom management abilities in his evaluation of me. I included a copy of this evaluation in my portfolio, under Standard Three, 'Learning Environments.'"

As Katie spoke, the interviewers passed her portfolio around the table, examining documents and making notes.

After several other questions and more examination of her portfolio, the personnel superintendent said, "Ms. Smith, you were one of several candidates for this position with a well-organized portfolio. Your verbal responses to our questions were excellent but so were those of other candidates. However, your portfolio was unique because it enabled you to support those responses with concrete examples of your knowledge and experience. Your electronic portfolio is also impressive, not only because it shows your abilities with computer technology, but also because it gives us a quick and convenient way to find your documents. Other candidates for this position had portfolios—even electronic ones—but yours was the only one organized around national teaching standards to show your capabilities in the teaching behaviors that we think are important. We are all very impressed. I think you'll make a fine addition to our district teaching faculty."

The preceding scenario makes evident how imperative it is that, as a prospective teacher, you are able to demonstrate your teaching competence to others in concrete ways. Teaching jobs are highly competitive, and therefore creative ways of presenting yourself are essential.

However, prospective employers are not the only ones who will be holding you accountable for proving your competence. State departments of education are increasing requirements for compelling evidence of performance before issuing teacher certification. Most states now have established standards that teacher candidates must meet for certification. In addition, in 1987, the National Board for Professional Teaching Standards was formed for the purpose of setting standards for the teaching profession, thus offering a voluntary national teaching certificate. Furthermore, many teacher education programs are utilizing measurements of performance as an alternative for evaluating preservice teachers' progress in their professional training. Once you obtain a teaching job, you will be periodically evaluated and held accountable for utilizing exemplary teaching practices throughout your professional career.

Traditionally, assessments such as test scores and transcript grades have been used to evaluate teachers. However, you will find that these types of assessments do not necessarily reflect the range of abilities that true professionals possess. Teachers are justifiably concerned that assessments and accountability requirements be authentic, broad based, and impartial. As a professional, you will want all of your knowledge and experience to be taken into account when you are evaluated.

One characteristic of excellent teachers is that they learn from every experience and every person they meet. They seek ongoing professional training to refine their practice. They remain current about educational research. They read professional journals and books, attend workshops, and interact with colleagues in order to benefit from the experience of others. They ask endless questions of other people and really listen to the answers. They try new ideas, reflect on the results, and then discard or adapt the ideas. Often they keep reflective journals. When they travel, they look for opportunities to learn all they can about other places. They volunteer in the community, getting to know its people, values, and agencies. When they join groups, they tend to be the ones who go to the meetings and do the work on committees.

Although teachers know that all these forms of experience have contributed to their becoming effective professionals, most would find it difficult to demonstrate to others exactly how these various experiences have fit into their pattern of professional growth. As you embark on your professional journey, you will probably find that you, too, have many valuable skills and experiences that are difficult to convey in a single test score or course grade. Because these skills and experiences are part of your growing competencies, it is important that you are able to convey information about them to others.

A professional portfolio can help. It can be a tool that enables you to make sense out of myriad experiences. It can also bring into focus a clear picture of yourself as a growing, changing professional. Equally as significant, it can be a convincing, effective vehicle for you to demonstrate to others in a meaningful way the skills and knowledge you have gained in something as complex as teaching.

WHAT IS A PORTFOLIO?

A portfolio is an organized, goal-driven documentation of your professional growth and competence in the complex act called teaching. It is a collection of documents that provides tangible evidence of the wide range of performances, essential knowledge, critical dispositions, and teaching experiences that you possess as a growing professional. What's more, documents in the portfolio are self-selected, reflecting your individuality and autonomy. Therefore, a portfolio is not merely a file of course projects and assignments, nor is it a scrapbook of teaching memorabilia.

There are actually two kinds of portfolios that you will be developing: a working portfolio and a presentation portfolio. A working portfolio is characterized by your ongoing systematic collection of selected work in courses and evidence of community activities. This collection forms a framework for self-assessment and goal setting. Later, you develop a presentation portfolio by winnowing your collection to samples of your work that best reflect your competence, individuality, and creativity as a professional educator.

What Is a Working Portfolio?

A working portfolio contains unabridged versions of the documents you have carefully selected to portray your professional growth. It is always much larger than a presentation portfolio. For example, it might contain entire reflective journals, complete units, unique teacher-made materials, and a collection of videos of your teaching. Working portfolios are often stored in a combination of electronic storage devices, notebooks, and even boxes.

What Is a Presentation Portfolio?

A presentation portfolio is compiled for the expressed purpose of giving others an effective and easy-to-read portrait of your professional competence. A presentation portfolio is selective and streamlined because other people usually do not have the time to review all the material in your working portfolio. This holds true whether it is a paper-based portfolio or an electronic one.

If you have chosen to create a paper-based portfolio, we recommend the use of a notebook, in which you insert only the most pertinent documents needed to showcase your abilities. If you have decided to create an electronic portfolio, you will find that it is easier to include a greater number and variety of documents; however, you will need to be sure to catalog them distinctly and accurately on your electronic storage device.

In making a presentation portfolio, you will find that less is more. For example, because you would be unlikely to take all your teacher-made learning materials to an interview, you might rely on either paper or digital photographs. If you have a video of your classroom teaching, make sure it is well edited and annotated, and then insert it into a pocket of your paper-based portfolio or add it to your electronic portfolio. If you have a large project that you wish to include in your portfolio, you can simply edit it for an electronic portfolio, but it may be necessary to streamline it to sample pages only for a paper-based portfolio.

The working portfolio and the presentation portfolio differ in that all documents in a presentation portfolio should be preceded by an explanation of the importance or relevance of each document so that the reviewer understands the context of your work.

HOW DO I ORGANIZE MY PORTFOLIO?

There is one essential way in which working portfolios and presentation portfolios are alike. From their inception, both need to have a well-established organizational system. There is no one standard way to organize a portfolio, but to be effective it must have a system of organization that is understandable and meaningful to you and other educators. We suggest organizing your portfolio around a set of goals you are trying to achieve. This makes sense when one of your purposes for a portfolio is to demonstrate to others that you are achieving success in meeting standards set for excellence in the teaching profession.

Many professional organizations have set goals for the teachers of the twenty-first century. These organizations include state departments of education, professional societies such as the National Association for the Education of Young Children or the National Council of Teachers of Mathematics, interagency groups, and university schools of education. Appendix A provides website addresses for many professional organizations concerned with standards for teaching. The professional goals established by these organizations are called by a variety of names, including *standards, principles, performance domains, outcomes, propositions,* and *competencies.* They are all attempts to reflect the knowledge, performances, and dispositions that define excellent teachers and therefore are goals for you to achieve.

You should become familiar with a number of documents that outline sets of standards for your discipline, state, and university department. As you study these standards, choose or adapt a set of goals that makes sense to you in your particular situation. Regardless of the goals or standards that you choose, everything collected for your portfolio should be organized around the chosen goal statements. Chapter 3 gives you more details on how to do this.

The sample goals or standards used in this text are principles established by the Interstate Teacher Assessment and Support Consortium (InTASC).[1] These standards were chosen because of their general applicability for teachers of all disciplines and all levels, preschool to grade twelve. It is apparent that engaging in the development of a portfolio organized around a set of goals or standards will greatly facilitate your growth and achievement in the goals identified. Figure 1.1 shows the InTASC standards.

WHAT EVIDENCE SHOULD I INCLUDE IN MY PORTFOLIO?

For every standard, you will include artifacts that demonstrate that you have met this standard. An artifact is tangible evidence of knowledge that is gained, skills that are mastered, values that are clarified, or dispositions and attitudes that are characteristic of you. Artifacts cannot conclusively prove the attainment of knowledge, performances, or dispositions, but they provide indicators of achieved competence. For example, lesson and unit plans are pieces of evidence that might provide strong indications of your ability to plan curriculum or use a variety of teaching strategies. A video of your teaching might be a convincing indicator of your ability to manage and motivate a group of students. The same artifact may document more than one standard. Chapter 5 will describe sixty-five possibilities for portfolio artifacts. At first, you will collect many artifacts. Later, you will need to place artifacts selectively within each of the standards. Those artifacts that represent your growth and very best professional work should be included as evidence in your professional portfolio. Ask yourself: Would I be proud to have my future employer and peer group see this? Is this an example of what my future professional work might look like? Does this represent what I stand for as a professional educator? If not, what can I do to revise or rearrange my artifacts so that they represent my best efforts?

WHO IS THE AUDIENCE FOR MY PORTFOLIO?

Information contained in the portfolio will be of interest to individuals who will be assessing your performance and measuring your accountability. While you are a preservice teacher, university faculty and advisors will review your portfolio. Moreover, your portfolio will be an excellent way for you to introduce yourself to cooperating teachers and administrators during

---

[1]Interstate Teacher Assessment and Support Consortium (InTASC). (April 2011). *Model core teaching standards: A resource for state dialogue.* Washington, DC: Council of Chief State School Officers.

Standard #1: Learner Development

The teacher understands how learners grow and develop, recognizing that patterns of learning and development vary individually within and across the cognitive, linguistic, social, emotional, and physical areas, and designs and implements developmentally appropriate and challenging learning experiences.

Standard #2: Learning Differences

The teacher uses understanding of individual differences and diverse cultures and communities to ensure inclusive learning environments that enable each learner to meet high standards.

Standard #3: Learning Environments

The teacher works with others to create environments that support individual and collaborative learning, and that encourage positive social interaction, active engagement in learning, and self motivation.

Standard #4: Content Knowledge

The teacher understands the central concepts, tools of inquiry, and structures of the discipline(s) he or she teaches and creates learning experiences that make these aspects of the discipline accessible and meaningful for learners to assure mastery of the content.

Standard #5: Application of Content

The teacher understands how to connect concepts and use differing perspectives to engage learners in critical thinking, creativity, and collaborative problem solving related to authentic local and global issues.

Standard #6: Assessment

The teacher understands and uses multiple methods of assessment to engage learners in their own growth, to monitor learner progress, and to guide the teacher's and learner's decision making.

Standard #7: Planning for Instruction

The teacher plans instruction that supports every student in meeting rigorous learning goals by drawing upon knowledge of content areas, curriculum, cross-disciplinary skills, and pedagogy, as well as knowledge of learners and the community context.

Standard #8: Instructional Strategies

The teacher understands and uses a variety of instructional strategies to encourage learners to develop deep understanding of content areas and their connections, and to build skills to apply knowledge in meaningful ways.

Standard #9: Professional Learning and Ethical Practice

The teacher engages in ongoing professional learning and uses evidence to continually evaluate his/her practice, particularly the effects of his/her choices and actions on others (learners, families, other professionals, and the community), and adapts practice to meet the needs of each learner.

Standard #10: Leadership and Collaboration

The teacher seeks appropriate leadership roles and opportunities to take responsibility for student learning, to collaborate with learners, families, colleagues, other school professionals, and community members to ensure learner growth, and to advance the profession.

FIGURE 1.1   InTASC Model Core Teaching Standards   *Source:* Interstate Teacher Assessment and Support Consortium (InTASC) (April, 2011). *Model core teaching standards: A resource for state dialogue.* Washington, DC: Council of Chief State School Officers.

field experiences and student teaching. During job interviews, your portfolio is likely to be reviewed by superintendents, principals, teachers, and in some cases even school-board members. As you begin your teaching career, your portfolio will be a helpful vehicle for mentors, in-service education coordinators, and other colleagues. In some school districts, supervisory staff charting ongoing career development or making tenure and promotion decisions rely on teaching portfolios. There is also a good possibility that your portfolio will one day be used to facilitate licensing by professional organizations, state agencies, or national consortiums. Most important, the portfolio provides you, the author, with an informative and accurate picture of your professional development and growth.

HOW MIGHT I USE MY PORTFOLIO?

In this chapter, you have been introduced to a very motivating reason for you to commit time, energy, and thought to developing a portfolio: You will have a high-impact, authentic product by which your professional competence can be judged by others. Before you read later chapters, which will provide you with detailed steps and examples for developing a portfolio, you might reflect on other ways besides interviews and certification requirements that you can use your portfolio to your best advantage.

As you engage in portfolio development, you will find that you will gain a much clearer picture of yourself as an emerging professional. Your portfolio will provide a record of quantitative and qualitative growth over time in your selected goal areas or standards. You will have in hand a trail of evidence of your progress in each of your teaching standards. This will give you a gratifying sense of accomplishment and pride and will help you increase your confidence in your professional abilities.

As you review this record of your professional growth, you will also gain a vision of the big picture. You will more fully understand who you want to be as a professional (as defined by the standards that you choose). Then, as you organize selected artifacts around these standards, you will begin to discern a pattern of how your various course assignments and out-of-class experiences fit into this big picture and contribute to your development.

As you gain more self-understanding, your portfolio will empower you to assume more control over your own future learning. You will be well equipped to collaborate with professors in individualizing assignments or with advisors in planning courses of study, if you are still in a preservice program. You will have a greatly expanded résumé to introduce yourself to cooperating teachers and administrators in student teaching, field experiences, or employment. You and your supervisors now have a tool for determining the most appropriate teaching experiences for you. When you reflect on the portrait your portfolio provides, you will be well positioned to set realistic and meaningful goals for yourself. Choices that you make in your coursework, field work, or self-initiated learning opportunities will now have a meaningful focus.

In addition, a university program may use the portfolio as a way to keep preservice teachers and faculty focused on goals or standards valued by the program. Preservice teachers will continually reflect on the standards as they develop portfolios that provide an authentic and meaningful way to be assessed professionally. Portfolios will provide faculty members with evidence of their effectiveness in preparing preservice teachers to meet selected standards. Portfolios can help with program evaluation, and they can bring to light the need for new courses, revised course syllabi, or policy changes.

It should now be clear what a portfolio is, what it includes, who would be interested in seeing it, and why having a professional portfolio is of value. Now you are ready to look at portfolio development in a more specific way.

TRY THIS

Writing an Autobiographical Sketch

A good way to start your portfolio is with a one-page autobiographical sketch or self-introduction. This might be in the form of a written narrative or a letter. This piece should provide the readers of your portfolio with some information about you that is not readily apparent from a résumé or even from your collection of artifacts. You can consider several possibilities as you write this. Think about the following categories and questions because they may help you compose your autobiographical sketch.

Why You Chose to Become a Teacher
- Have you had a lifelong dream of becoming a teacher?
- What set of circumstances in your life brought you into the teaching field?
- Who influenced you most as you were growing up or as you were making decisions about your life's work?

Your Personal Attributes
- What attributes do you have that would make you a good teacher?
- Are you a warm and nurturing person who is especially encouraging to others?
- Do you have a professional demeanor and businesslike attitude?
- Do you hold high expectations for your own success and for the success of your students?
- Have you overcome some personal obstacles that would help you empathize with students who must do the same?
- Have you had unique experiences or travels that would enhance your students' experiences in your classroom?

Your Long-Term Goals and Ambitions
- Where do you see yourself in five years? In ten years?
- What ambitions do you have as an educator?
- How will your goals and ambitions make you a better teacher?

2

Guidelines for Assembling Your Portfolio

HOW TO USE THIS CHAPTER

Creating a portfolio takes time and personal reflection. As stated in Chapter 1, the process of developing a portfolio begins early in your professional career, when you start to collect documents and pieces of your work that exemplify your capabilities as a teacher. This collection, called the working portfolio, will be extensive; it will contain everything you have done that you judge to be worthy of saving. Eventually, you will need to produce a presentation portfolio. This is for the purpose of showcasing only portions of your work for a prospective employer or certification officer. The presentation portfolio is streamlined: Only the most pertinent material for the position is organized and displayed. Both types of portfolios are organized in the same manner: Documents are categorized by standards that you have adopted. These standards are goals that will guide you throughout your teacher preparation work, your career, or both. This chapter will give you some practical information on putting together both types of portfolios. See Chapter 7 for suggestions on constructing an electronic portfolio.

The first section of the chapter contains information to help you organize your collection of documents for a working portfolio. This will be an ongoing project as you complete your teacher education program or prepare for certification. The second section is designed to help you produce a presentation portfolio that is uniquely yours, at the same time documenting important information that will be examined by prospective employers or certification officers. We have included questions that you may have about assembling your portfolio. The answers provide guidelines that are important; however, feel free to use your own creativity in developing a portfolio that portrays you as an individual as well as a professional educator.

CREATING THE WORKING PORTFOLIO

Where Do I Start?

Choose a way to store your documents. The working portfolio will contain a multitude of artifacts, many of which will be cumbersome. Decide how you want to house your artifacts. The portfolio needs to be easily accessible, expandable, and organized. You may want to use a large file box. Office supply stores carry cardboard banker's boxes, which are easily assembled and easy to carry around. You can put all your artifacts in one box, with files dividing it into sections. If you prefer, you can use several smaller boxes, one for each standard you are documenting. Other options are to use a large notebook that can be divided into sections or a file drawer in a cabinet that has plenty of space for several folders. Rather than always storing hard copies, you might opt to save many documents in digital format on a flash drive or on your computer's hard drive. Preservice teacher education programs may require the specific use of a software program or online portfolio development system.

Consider the types of artifacts you will be saving when making this decision. Will you be using a number of DVDs or videos? Will you be making teaching materials you will want to save? Will you be taking photographs of projects? Do you tend to write lengthy papers? These types of artifacts require space as well as special types of handling when organizing and storing them for long periods of time.

How Do I Choose a Set of Standards?

If you are a preservice teacher, you may well be assigned a particular set of standards to use when developing your portfolio. Many schools of education have developed or adapted their own sets of goals for their students. Some use the standards set by their particular state department of education. Other programs rely on standards developed by professional societies such as the Council for Exceptional Children (CEC). A good number of teacher education programs use the InTASC core standards for teachers because of the standards' universal applicability to teachers of every subject and age group. However, there are many preservice teachers who have the opportunity to choose the set of standards for organizing their professional portfolios. If you are an inservice teacher, it is even more likely that you will have the freedom to choose a set of standards for guiding portfolio work. Chapter 3 will offer an account of an inservice teacher's search for appropriate standards.

Whether or not you are assigned a set of standards to use, you should become familiar with all the professional standards available for your particular specialization. You will get specific help with this task in Chapter 3. As you review several sources, you will likely notice that there is a great deal of overlap in these sets of standards due to a great deal of agreement in the profession on what characterizes excellent teaching. The educators who have developed these sets of standards have based them on sound educational theory, principles of best practice, and research.

How Do I Document the Standards?

CREATE A FILING SYSTEM.   Your portfolio will contain several sections, each of which will correspond to a standard you have adopted. In the examples provided in this book, each section will reflect one of the ten standards outlined by InTASC. These standards are descriptions of teacher behaviors agreed upon by a group of educators in the consortium and were developed to be compatible with other national standards for certification.

Your portfolio needs to document that you have indeed met your chosen goals. Therefore, organize your portfolio in such a way that these standards are easily identified. If you are using a file box or expanding file for your working portfolio, create a file or section for each standard. You may want to color-code the files to facilitate easier management. If you are using a notebook to house your working portfolio, the best way to do this is to include tab pages for each standard, dividing your portfolio into as many sections as there are standards. Or, you may wish to maintain an electronic folder for each standard.

EXAMINE THE POSSIBILITIES FOR DOCUMENTATION.   Study the suggestions and examples in this manual. Sample standard statements, along with real-life examples, are listed and explained in Chapter 4. In Chapter 5, many possible artifacts are listed that could be used to document any set of standards. They have been defined and explained so that you can get some idea of what is meant by terms such as *video scenario critiques* or *theme studies,* and you can also see the possibilities for documenting standards. Check your files for any of these artifacts and save them. Many of your artifacts probably reflect class assignments given in your methods classes. However, you may want to create artifacts. For example, you may have not written a philosophy statement, but you have a very clear idea of your philosophy of education. Therefore, composing one for the purpose of including it in the portfolio would be a wise idea. You may also need to add to artifacts you already have. Suppose you attended a professional meeting or lecture but did not write a reaction paper or take notes. Now is a good time to write a brief critique of what you saw and heard and add it to your file for the portfolio.

BECOME A PACK RAT.   If you have not already done so, begin collecting. Organize your file box, cabinet, electronic storage devices, or notebook and start putting examples of class assignments and other artifacts in appropriate categories right away. This is necessary because you will want to see if there are any standards for which you do not have artifacts, something that is discussed in the next section. Remember that you can use an artifact in more than one section because several types of artifacts may document more than one standard. If this happens, photocopy the artifact and highlight the part that specifically addresses the standard. One note of caution: Use this photocopying and highlighting idea sparingly. Duplicating too many artifacts will make your portfolio look as if you do not use a variety of experiences.

As you file each of your artifacts under a standard, make brief notes about why you have filed the document under that particular standard. These notes can be used later when you are ready to create your presentation portfolio. At that time, you will need to write a rationale for each artifact. This is a brief statement that explains why the artifact

Standard One—Case Study
- Shows how a child's language developed from infancy
- Written over a three-month period
- Identifies some stages of language development
- Shows how the child learned several new words

FIGURE 2.1 Example of a Note Card to Attach to the Artifact when Filing in the Working Portfolio

you chose for the standard is appropriate and how the artifact showcases your competence in that area. From the standard statement, use specific descriptors that will jar your memory and connect the artifact to the standard. You may want to write these notes on an index card and clip the card to the document. Figure 2.1 shows an example of notes written for a case study that could be used to document InTASC Standard One.

LOOK FOR HOLES. Standards that are not well documented by your artifacts will become evident as you collect and categorize materials. Keep the standards in mind as you take other courses or participate in professional activities. Whenever you have assignment choices, such as journal article critiques to write or projects to complete in your university coursework, think about the standards you need to work on. Consider how you can make this assignment document your "missing standard." Look for meetings to attend, journals to read or to which you can subscribe, organizations to join, extra-credit assignments to complete, community activities for which to volunteer, personal diaries to write, or any number of activities that can be recorded and included in your portfolio. You may also want to ask your professors for guidance in this area. See if they have suggestions for ways to make your class assignments document a particular standard while at the same time completing the requirements for their courses.

CREATING THE PRESENTATION PORTFOLIO

Why Create Another Portfolio?

At various stages in your professional career, when you want to showcase your abilities to someone else, you will need a presentation portfolio. You should determine the collection of documents by the audience reviewing the presentation portfolio. For example, in a preservice teacher education program, the audience might be faculty and cooperating teachers. Later, you will tailor a presentation portfolio specifically to a job or a type of teaching certification that you are seeking. As an experienced teacher, you might use your presentation portfolio for national board certification, mentoring, managing your own professional growth, or advancing within the profession. Chapter 6 elaborates on these uses of presentation portfolios.

How Do I Prepare the Presentation Portfolio?

USE A STORAGE DEVICE THAT WORKS FOR YOU. For your presentation portfolio, you can experiment with many types of storage devices such as notebooks, expanding files, folders, flash drives, compact disks (CDs), or portfolio cases. Consider the types of artifacts you have collected. If you have electronic documents that are stored on videos or computer disks, you will need to format them so they are easily accessible and logically organized. When using a hard-copy portfolio, your reader should be able to open and read it without struggling with pages, binders, or pockets. Therefore, use a container that is large enough to house all your documents. Most people choose a large notebook. Generally, two- or three-inch three-ring binders are fine. A professional look is important. Browse through an office supply store for your notebook. Many stores carry notebooks with a plastic insert cover that you can personalize. Pockets for storage of electronic documents are also available and can be inserted easily into most types of notebooks. One note of caution: Do not use a notebook that is too big, or your portfolio will look empty.

IDENTIFY THE STANDARDS.   Remember that your prospective employer or certification officer might not know what each of the standard titles means. As with the working portfolio, you will need to label each section with an abbreviated title for the standard as well as a copy of the entire standard statement.

BE SELECTIVE IN CHOOSING ARTIFACTS.   As in the working portfolio, you will gather artifacts that document your abilities in each of the standards you have adopted. However, most reviewers do not have a great deal of time to peruse portfolios and are interested in only the most pertinent information about your abilities. This means you must be selective in what you choose for the presentation portfolio. Two or three artifacts in each section are all you need. Choose artifacts that exemplify the type of position or certificate you are seeking. For example, if you are interviewing for a first-grade teaching position, select as many examples of your work in the area of early childhood education as possible.

WRITE A RATIONALE.   In each section of your portfolio, you will insert various artifacts that document your proficiency and experience for that standard. However, readers of your portfolio will not necessarily know why you included these particular artifacts. Therefore, you need to include a rationale for each artifact in the notebook. Type a brief statement explaining your justification for including this artifact in the portfolio for this particular standard. This statement should be no longer than one page. Make sure you explain why this is an example of your best work for this specific standard. Your rationale should show the reader what you are capable of doing to meet the standard. Be specific about showcasing your abilities. (This is difficult for some people; they feel as if they are bragging.) Do not simply summarize the document. When writing a rationale, answer the following questions. A well-written rationale answers all five questions; however, the order in which you answer these questions is not important.

> *What?*   What is the experience reflected in this document?
>
> *What?*   What is the artifact?
>
> *So what?*   What does this work say about my growing competence?
>
> *Where and why?*   Under which standard is it filed? Why there?
>
> *Now what?*   What will I do differently in the future? How will the skills I've gained transfer to new experiences?

SAMPLE RATIONALE PAGE

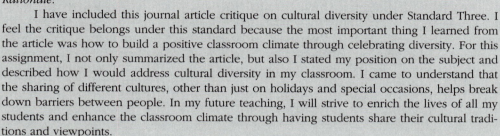

Artifact for Standard Three: Learning Environments

Name of Artifact: Journal Article Critique
Date: May 2, 2012
Course: EDE 201—Foundations of Education
Rationale:
   I have included this journal article critique on cultural diversity under Standard Three. I feel the critique belongs under this standard because the most important thing I learned from the article was how to build a positive classroom climate through celebrating diversity. For this assignment, I not only summarized the article, but also I stated my position on the subject and described how I would address cultural diversity in my classroom. I came to understand that the sharing of different cultures, other than just on holidays and special occasions, helps break down barriers between people. In my future teaching, I will strive to enrich the lives of all my students and enhance the classroom climate through having students share their cultural traditions and viewpoints.

FIGURE 2.2   Example of a Rationale Page for a University Course Assignment

To organize your portfolio and make artifacts and rationales clearly identifiable, add a rationale page for each artifact you include. This page lists the name of the artifact and the date it was written. If applicable, list the course number for the class in which you completed the assignment. Then, type the rationale statement for the artifact. Figures 2.2 and 2.3 show examples of rationale pages.

PRESENT YOUR ARTIFACTS PROFESSIONALLY.   Remember that this portfolio will represent you as a professional, often in your absence. You will want to make sure your first impression is a good one. Therefore, carefully consider all that goes in your notebook, file, or electronic portfolio. Listed below are questions to ask yourself as you check your work.

1. Have I been careful to present only my own work? (For example, you should not include handouts prepared by someone else for training you've attended.) Have I shared credit for work I've done collaboratively with others?
2. Are spelling and grammar in standard English?
3. Is all work typed? (The only exceptions to typed work would be artifacts such as journals, students' papers, or observation logs that were not originally typed.)
4. Is everything about my overall presentation consistent? Are lines on my rationale pages either single spaced or double spaced consistently throughout?
5. Is my work neat? Have I used the same font style and size throughout?
6. Is my organization easy to follow? Do I have a table of contents that clearly identifies all parts of the portfolio?
7. Have I maintained confidentiality throughout?

How Do I Make the Presentation Portfolio Unique?

Your presentation portfolio will be unique because it reflects your abilities, strengths, and professionalism. No one else will have a portfolio like yours because you have written all

Sample Rationale Page

Artifact for Standard Nine: Professional Learning and Ethical Practice

Name of Artifact: Who's Who Among American Teachers Selection Letter
Date: March, 2012
Rationale:

   I was recently selected into Who's Who Among American Teachers. I received this letter of selection at a time in my career when I needed some encouragement. The nomination letter was written by one of my students. I placed this document under Standard Nine because it helped me to step back and take a look at what I was doing and what I needed to be doing.

   I had what seemed to me one class of rather lazy and apathetic students. I was having a difficult time getting them to do their work or even come to class. I was beginning to get a serious case of "Why do I do this?" when this letter appeared in my mailbox. I read the letter several times and then thought about what I had done to make such an impression on this particular student. I thought about the class that she was in and how active and involved the students in it always were. Her recognition of my teaching efforts meant so much to me and gave me a new goal—to do everything I could to make the class I was struggling with now feel as she did. I began looking at our units with renewed enthusiasm and the desire to live up to the high praise that I had received. I began preparing new activities designed to make these students want to be in class and do the work. By the end of the semester, their grades had greatly improved, along with their attitudes (and mine).

   This one letter helped me realize that I need to constantly work to live up to this award. When I start getting tired or frustrated, I can look back on the impact I had on this one student and feel reenergized and ready to do what it takes to affect someone else in the same way. It was as if I had lost my purpose for teaching somewhere in the content, and Natasha found it, dusted it off, and handed it back to me, as good as new.

FIGURE 2.3   Example of a Rationale Page Written by a High School Teacher

the documents. Others will be able to see very quickly what you know about teaching and what you believe about education. Listed in the following subsections are ways to make the portfolio more personalized.

BE CREATIVE.   You may wish to add touches of creativity such as pertinent artwork, photographs, video clips, or famous quotations. Other embellishments include borders, clip art, icons, graphic organizers, and captions for photographs. Your rationale pages for each of the artifacts would be good places for these. You can also be creative with the cover or entry page of your portfolio, making sure to include all necessary identifying information. Another way to add creativity is to develop the portfolio around a theme. (One creative portfolio depicted its writer as a traveler on a journey down the road of professional life.) Whatever you do, keep embellishment simple. Although visual impact is important, overuse of photographs or decorated pages may detract from the professionalism of your documents. You do not want to detract from the work you are trying to showcase, nor do you want to appear as if you are trying to hide incompetence.

CREATE A PLACE FOR PERSONAL DATA.   As you move through various stages of your professional career, documents in your professional portfolio will change. Some documents, however, are beneficial at any stage. At the beginning of your portfolio, in a well-marked section, include important documents that serve as an introduction. Possibilities are:

1. Letter of introduction or preface to the portfolio
2. Your photograph
3. Biographical sketch
4. Résumé
5. Letters of recommendation
6. Transcripts
7. Student-teaching evaluations
8. Certification documents
9. Philosophy of education statement

CREATE A TABLE OF CONTENTS.   Once you have all the pieces to your presentation portfolio assembled, prepare a table of contents to aid your reviewers. The following is a sample table of contents for a portfolio built around InTASC standards.

Contents

Preface

About the Author

Philosophy of Education

Personal Data
  Résumé
  Letters of Recommendation
  Transcripts
  Student-Teaching Evaluations

Artifacts for Standard One—Learner Development
  Case Study of a Seventh-Grade Boy
  Observation Report on Characteristics of Third Graders

Artifacts for Standard Two—Learning Differences
  Self-Evaluation of Teaching a Talented and Gifted Group
  Letter of Recommendation on Coaching Multilevel Swimmers

Artifacts for Standard Three—Learning Environments
  Behavior Analysis after Implementing a Reward System
  Summary of Workshops on Proactive Classroom Management

Artifacts for Standard Four—Content Knowledge
  Science Unit on Geology
  Research Paper on Medieval Times

Artifacts for Standard Five—Application of Content
  Multidisciplinary Unit on World War II
  Video of Student Presentations of Emergency Plans for Communities with High Earthquake Frequency

Artifacts for Standard Six—Assessment
    Performance Assessment for Unit on Pond Life
    Chapter Test in Social Studies

Artifacts for Standard Seven —Planning for Instruction
    Lesson Plan on Money
    Thematic Unit Plan on Natural Disasters

Artifacts for Standard Eight—Instructional Strategies
    Cooperative Learning Activity
    Discovery Lesson on Immigration

Artifacts for Standard Nine—Professional Learning and Ethical Practice
    Outstanding Student Teacher of the Year Certificate
    Pictures of Afterschool Fitness Program

Artifacts for Standard Ten—Leadership and Collaboration
    Homework Assignments Encouraging Parent Involvement
    Participation Log for Parent–Teacher Association

A Final Word: Reflections on the Past, Goals for the Future

Remember, the portfolio portrays you as both an individual and a professional. It shows evidence of your personal insights into your experiences and that you have reflected on what you can do. In short, it is your showcase; use it to your advantage.

TRY THIS

Writing Your First Rationale

Writing a rationale for the first time can be somewhat intimidating. That need not be the case. In fact, rationales have a predictable pattern that makes their composition easier. Once you understand the pattern and the basic questions that rationales answer, you will write them with greater ease. Try writing a rough draft of your first rationale by following these steps in the order presented. This exercise will help you become acquainted with the construction of rationales.

1. Select an experience or a class assignment that you want to showcase in your portfolio because you value the learning that it provided to you.
2. Now you will use the questions on page 13 to help you write your first rationale. Look at the first question: **"What is the experience reflected in this document?"** Describe the assignment or experience clearly so that it can be understood by a reader of your portfolio who is unfamiliar with your work and your class assignments.
3. Think about your response to the second "what" question: **"What is the artifact?"** Will you use a letter of recommendation, a lesson plan, a summary, or perhaps a research paper to document this experience? Remember that an experience can be documented with more than one artifact. Make a note of the artifact or collection of artifacts that you intend to use.
4. Now make a list that answers the third question: **"So what?"** Write down all the skills, competencies, or understandings that you gained through this experience. How did this experience or class assignment benefit you and better prepare you for teaching? For some experiences, you will have one major gain or outcome; for other, more complex experiences such as field experiences in classrooms, you will have many competencies that you gained.

5. The next question is: **"Where and why?"** Under what standard will you file this artifact? Why there? To answer these questions, you need to review your list of outcomes in Step 4 to see how they relate to the standards you are using. Put a circle around the most important thing you learned from this experience. You should file your work under the standard that best corresponds to the most important benefit of this experience, even if the experience provided a host of other benefits.

6. Finally, think about the last question: **"Now what?"** Make notes of ways that you can use what you learned from this experience in your future teaching experiences.

7. Using the notes from Steps 2–6, write one or two paragraphs summarizing this information. *Remember, the order in which you address these guiding questions can vary in your rationales.* The important thing is that your paragraphs answer all the questions in this list.

8. You are now ready to create the heading for the rationale. The important thing to remember when naming the artifact in the heading is to use a simple, straightforward title that most clearly communicates the nature of the document. It is also important to remember that you use the date the experience occurred, not the date the rationale was written.

For additional help with writing rationales, review the two sample rationales in this chapter and the ten sample rationales in Chapter 4.

3

Choosing Standards for Your Portfolio

WHAT ARE STANDARDS?

Have you been asked to create a standards-based portfolio? If so, it makes sense to understand the nature of standards. What is a standard? *Merriam-Webster Online* lists nine definitions of the word! The third of these defines *standard* as "something established by authority, custom, or general consent as a model or example." Thus, teaching standards are the requirements by which you will be judged, evaluated, or assessed throughout your teaching career, starting with your work at a university as you prepare to become a teacher. Getting to know the standards that are the criteria for your work is a prudent way to begin developing your professional portfolio.

Why Do We Have Standards for Teachers?

Since 1983, with the publication of the federal report *A Nation at Risk*, much work has been done in a variety of places to reform public schools. One type of reform has focused on defining quality teachers. Generally, effective teachers are defined as those who enable their students to achieve, grow, and develop optimally. Policy makers, educators, and educational organizations have asked questions such as:

- What knowledge must an effective teacher possess?
- What skills does an effective teacher demonstrate?
- What are the personal attributes that an effective teacher must have?

Various educational and governing groups have attempted to answer these questions by creating sets of standards for teachers. Examples of these groups are organizations that guide the professional development of teachers, state governments, school districts, and universities.

What Are the Types of Standards for Teachers?

As we have mentioned before, standards are identified by various names; they are also called *principles, competencies,* or *propositions.* Some sets of standards were written for teachers of a certain discipline, such as the standards developed by the National Council of Teachers of English (NCTE) or the National Council for the Social Studies (NCSS). Some standards were written for teachers who serve a particular population. For example, the National Association for the Education of Young Children (NAEYC) offers standards for teachers and caregivers of children from birth to age eight, and the CEC provides guidelines for teachers of students with learning challenges.

Some sets of standards were written in more general terms to define the knowledge and skills needed by all teachers, regardless of the population they serve or the disciplines they teach. InTASC wrote a set of this type of standards for teachers, which you learned about in Chapter 1 of this book. In addition to the model core standards used in this text, InTASC has translated these into model standards in elementary education, social studies, mathematics, English language arts, science, special education, foreign languages, and the arts. For more experienced teachers, the National Board for Professional Teaching Standards (NBPTS) offers complex advanced standards in a variety of certification areas that lead to national certification. You'll read about those in Chapter 6. These are just a few of the standards that are available to teachers, and they are updated periodically. As you can see, there is great variety in the standards that teachers can choose from, all with the purpose of providing criteria for excellence in teaching.

WHAT IS STANDARDS-BASED EDUCATION?

Standards-based education is a way of teaching that uses established content standards as a means of measuring how well students do at mastering the content. This is the way teachers are now required to teach at most elementary, middle, and high schools—they are given standards for each of the subject areas and are expected to teach so that their students meet these standards. The same idea holds for educating teachers. Colleges of education are provided standards created by groups such as the ones previously described or by their state governments, and they use these standards as guidelines for preparing teachers. Most university programs are governed by an accrediting agency, which requires that teacher candidates demonstrate their abilities in at least one set of standards. These standards provide a way of assessing teacher candidates to be sure that they possess the knowledge and skills deemed necessary to teach a particular grade level or subject area and to ensure that the university program is meeting the standards for preparing future teachers.

WHAT IS A STANDARDS-BASED PORTFOLIO?

A standards-based portfolio is one organized around a defined set of standards. As you read in Chapter 2, this type of organization makes the portfolio more than a collection of your favorite work: It is documentation of your abilities in specific areas. It is dynamic because it changes over time and circumstance. For example, you may document InTASC standards while you are going to college to learn to be a teacher; as you move forward in your teaching career, you may change your organization of documents to reflect the NBPTS that are applicable to the grade level or subject you teach and certification you hold.

All standards-based portfolios have this in common: These portfolios contain artifacts you have carefully selected that provide evidence of the performances, essential knowledge, and critical dispositions required of the standard. Thus, rather than simply collecting pictures of your favorite classroom experiences, you will be seeking experiences in the many components of teaching that are defined in the standards that apply to you. You will collect documents that showcase these experiences to others.

How Do I Select Standards That Apply to Me?

You may have mandated standards by which you will be assessed, or you may be creating a portfolio with little guidance. Regardless of the amount of structure provided by your college, university, or school district, it makes sense to find out what is expected of you. Many colleges of education now require teacher candidates to demonstrate their abilities as measured by a particular set of standards. Your university's school of education may have a written set of goals for you to achieve. If the state in which you live or attend college defines effective teaching, it is a good idea for you to find out how the state defines that term. It is also wise to find out which professional organizations have sets of standards that would apply to you. This knowledge of standards will guide you as you create your portfolio; what's more, your understanding of the way standards work reflects your professionalism.

Remember, knowing the standards that apply to you means more than merely memorizing the categories of teacher behaviors outlined in this set of standards. It means that you will develop a thorough understanding of the nature of teaching. As a professional educator, you should know how effective teaching is defined; moreover, it makes sense to know the various criteria by which you will be measured. All of these standards honor the complexity and challenges of your teaching responsibilities. They focus on the knowledge and skills needed to do the real, everyday work of teaching.

Let's imagine that you are an undergraduate in the state of Maine, preparing to teach special needs children. You would want to become familiar with the following: (1) the state's requirements as outlined in the ten Maine Initial Teaching Standards, (2) the standards developed by the CEC, (3) the InTASC core standards for teachers and associated special education subcategories, and (4) the goals and standards adopted by your university.

As another example, suppose you are an inservice teacher and that you teach second grade in Pennsylvania. You would want to carefully review (1) the Pennsylvania Department of Education PreK–4 Candidate Competencies, (2) standards provided by the NAEYC, (3) Danielson's Framework for Teaching and (4) the NBPTS for experienced early childhood teachers.

One thing you may notice is that many sets of standards are similar. That's because educators generally agree on the types of things that teachers ought to be able to do. When we first set out to establish a portfolio system at our university in 1996, we chose to adopt the InTASC core standards (1992 edition) as measures of our teacher candidates' abilities and as a way of assessing ourselves as faculty members. In 2011, the Council of Chief State School Officers (CCSSO) updated the core teaching standards, and they are generally recognized as the types of performances that teachers should demonstrate. Many other educational groups, in creating their own sets of standards, have used the InTASC standards as a springboard for their guidelines.

In this book, we focus on the use of InTASC standards for portfolio development. In Chapter 4, you will see explanations and examples of teaching scenarios, portfolio artifacts, and rationales, which will help you make decisions about how to document your experiences. If you decide to build your portfolio using a different set of standards, you will probably find it quite easy to determine a connection between those standards and the InTASC standards. A few organizations have made such correlations and have published them; a simple Internet search will help you find them.

Table 3.1 shows the titles of the ten InTASC standards, the ten standards adopted by the CEC, the five core propositions of the NBPTS, and the four domains of Danielson's Framework for Teaching. Note the similarities.

One Teacher's Portfolio Development

Let's look at an example of the decisions made by a teacher who developed her standards-based portfolio. Alicia has been teaching in Maryland for several years. When she began searching for her first teaching job, she created a standards-based portfolio organized around the InTASC core standards (1992 edition). At the time, it was not required by her college of education to develop a portfolio, but she used an earlier edition of this book as a guide to create one that would showcase her strengths as a new teacher. Now, after four years of high school teaching, she wants to reorganize her portfolio to better guide her future professional development. Most of this time she has taught general science and chemistry in culturally diverse schools and has worked with students who have multiple learning challenges. Her special interests are very broad: science education, brain development (neuroplasticity), educational therapy, outdoor education, learning disabilities, and curriculum development. She wants her portfolio to reflect these interests and document her growing competence in these areas, as well as her general teaching abilities. She wants a standards-based portfolio. She searched for the best standards for herself by reviewing these professional resources:

- InTASC Model Standards in Science
- InTASC Model Standards in Special Education
- American Chemical Society (ACS)
- National Science Teachers Association (NSTA)
- Association of Educational Therapists (AET)
- NBPTS (Adolescence and Young Adulthood/Science)
- NBTPS (Exceptional Needs Specialists)
- Maryland State Standards
- Standards for the county in Maryland where she teaches

Alicia's experience with portfolio development, using the 1992 InTASC standards, is shown in Figure 3.1.

A standards-based portfolio is one that is organized around a set of standards. There are many standards that outline the knowledge and skills that a teacher ought to possess,

TABLE 3.1   A Comparison of Four Sets of Standards

InTASC	CEC	NBPTS	Danielson FFT
Standard 1–Learner Development	Standard 1–Foundations	Proposition 1–Teachers are committed to students and their learning.	Domain One–Planning and Preparation
Standard 2–Learning Differences	Standard 2–Development and Characteristics of Learners		
Standard 3–Learning Environments	Standard 3–Individual Learning Differences	Proposition 2–Teachers know the subjects they teach and how to teach those subjects.	Domain Two–Classroom Environment
			Domain Three–Instruction
Standard 4–Content Knowledge	Standard 4–Instructional Strategies	Proposition 3–Teachers are responsible for managing and monitoring student learning.	Domain Four–Professional Responsibilities
Standard 5–Application of Content	Standard 5–Learning Environments and Social Interactions		
Standard 6–Assessment	Standard 6–Language	Proposition 4–Teachers think systematically about their practice and learn from experience.	
Standard 7–Planning for Instruction	Standard 7–Instructional Planning		
Standard 8–Instructional Strategies	Standard 8–Assessment	Proposition 5–Teachers are members of learning communities.	
Standard 9–Professional Learning and Ethical Practice	Standard 9–Professional and Ethical Practice		
Standard 10–Leadership and Collaboration	Standard 10–Collaboration		

according to the organization that created them. You may have a set of standards given to you for use in creating your portfolio, or you may need to choose standards on your own. Either way, as a professional, you will need to be familiar with the behaviors that make up a good teacher and to know what is expected of you by other professionals. Just as Alicia did, studying the standards that are most applicable to your teaching situation will help you do this. This comfort with standards will enable you to create or find documents that show your abilities in all of the appropriate standards that apply to you. In so doing, you will develop a standards-based portfolio that clearly shows others that you know how to teach.

After four years of teaching, I decided it was time to rethink the organization of my professional portfolio. I knew I wanted to keep my portfolio organized around standards, but I was unsure which standards would best enable me to portray my growing competence and my various interests in education and learning theory. The first thing I needed to do was determine what standards were available. Once I developed a list of specific organizations to search for standards, it was not difficult to find them. For example, doing an Internet search for "National Board Teaching Standards" quickly yielded the information I was seeking. Attempting more generic searches like "teaching standards" or "science teaching standards" did not result in the list of options that I needed. I found that it is much more effective to list first the appropriate organizations and then search for their standards under the name of the organization.

My search yielded standards I could place into three categories: those that were intended for educators to assess themselves and for others to assess educators; content standards for a subject matter; and requirements (courses and experience levels) to become a member of an organization.

Organizations that were not specifically geared toward educators, such as the Association of Educational Therapists (AET), were the least helpful in my quest for teaching standards. Their standards were more centered on requirements to join the organization and therefore were not something a portfolio could be built around.

The American Chemical Society (ACS) provided content standards that would be helpful to those developing a curriculum. In addition, I found content standards provided by the state and county in which I work. These content standards will be helpful to me as I continue to work on curriculum development or if I should want to showcase my abilities to present various topics adeptly. For the time being, however, I feel building my portfolio around content standards would be too specific for my needs.

The National Science Teachers Association (NSTA) offered standards for almost any need: teaching, professional development for teachers of science, science education assessment, science content, science education programs, and science education systems. The standards for teaching are highly appropriate to form the organizational structure for a portfolio. I feel certain that it would be beneficial for any science educator to read the more specific, related standards and other information given by NSTA to get a better overview of teaching secondary science.

In addition to NSTA, I found two other excellent sources for teaching standards that I most valued: InTASC standards and the National Board for Professional Teaching Standards (NBPTS). The InTASC ten core standards were the basis for my original portfolio. This time I looked closely at two sets of subject-specific standards developed by InTASC: Model Standards in Science and Model Standards in Special Education. I found that the science and the special education standards were fundamentally the same as the ten core teaching standards. They differed from the core standards in the implications and related standards. To adapt my portfolio to be more subject specific would require absolutely no change in the basic setup of the portfolio. It would be possible to address the general teaching standards and both of these two subject-specific standards in one portfolio without too much confusion. Looking at the subject-specific standards provided additional insight into what is important to showcase and what might be good artifacts to include to better illustrate my strengths and areas of interest.

At first glance, the NBPTS standards seemed very different from InTASC standards. NBPTS offers five broad propositions. After studying the subcategories to the propositions, however, I realized that the five propositions are just wider umbrellas that cover the same basic principles as InTASC, but for more experienced teachers. NBPTS also has subject-specific

(Continued)

FIGURE 3.1 Inservice Teacher's Perspective on Choosing Standards for Her Portfolio

standards for science teachers and exceptional needs specialists. These subject standards are very similar to each other but different from the core propositions.

As I reflected on my final choice for a set of standards, I considered that my career seems to be going in the direction of teaching science more than working with students with exceptional needs. While I have chosen to focus on science, the similarities between standards will allow me to simultaneously showcase my abilities to teach science and to work with all students in inclusive settings.

For two primary reasons I have decided to use the five NBPTS teaching propositions to organize my current portfolio work. The first reason is that I am looking into becoming nationally board certified in the next few years. Focusing my attention on these propositions might highlight areas I need to improve prior to following that path. The second reason is I like the more general standards at this point in my career. The specificity of the InTASC core standards was excellent for me as a new teacher. They gave me very focused guidelines as to what others might be looking for when hiring. They also helped me to see specific areas needing improvement during my first few years of teaching. As I have grown as an educator, however, I feel I do not need such specification anymore and will be better able to showcase my unique abilities and strengths with broader categories. The standards I will be using for my updated portfolio are (1) Teachers are committed to students and their learning, (2) Teachers know the subjects they teach and how to teach those subjects, (3) Teachers are responsible for managing and monitoring student learning, (4) Teachers think systematically about their practices and learn from experience, and (5) Teachers are members of learning communities.

FIGURE 3.1   *Continued*

TRY THIS

Comparing Sets of Standards

1. Use Appendix A to choose two or three professional organizations related to your teaching specialization. Locate standards for teachers on their websites. Print and/or save the relevant material.
2. Locate and print and/or save the InTASC standards for your specialization, if available.
3. Research and print and/or save any standards or goals set by your state department of education, your university, or the school district employing you.
4. If you are an inservice teacher, be sure to review, print and save relevant standards published by the NBPTS.
5. Now compare these sets of standards with each other and with the InTASC core standards. Try answering the following questions:

   - What overlap do you notice?
   - What unique perspectives can you find?
   - Choose one standard from InTASC. Look at all of the standards you've printed and/or saved to discover how that standard is addressed by all of the organizations.
   - How can studying various sets of standards help you to more fully understand the particular set of standards that you are using in your portfolio?

4

Organization of Portfolios Around Teaching Standards

HOW TO USE THIS CHAPTER

The art and science of teaching is a complex and challenging activity that cannot be totally and succinctly described by any set of goals, standards, or analysis of duties. However, for the purpose of charting and demonstrating professional growth through a portfolio, some system of categories is needed, imperfect though it may be.

For the purpose of providing a working example of a portfolio, we have chosen a set of standards or principles developed by the CCSSO that is called the InTASC Model Core Teaching Standards. In part we chose these standards because they are aligned with standards from many national professional associations and with the NBPTS. These InTASC Model Core Teaching Standards set expectations for excellent teaching practices across all grade levels and all subject areas. They provide worthy goals for beginning teachers and experienced teachers alike. Therefore, they have wide applicability. Furthermore, these standards have received wide acceptance and use.

If you choose to organize your portfolio around the InTASC core standards, you will find this chapter invaluable. Each of the ten standards is explained and depicted in a real-life scenario. Then you are shown a sample portfolio rationale that can be used with artifacts to document each standard. Therefore, you will be able to read each standard, understand what it means, and see it in practice.

If you are not using the InTASC core standards but have adopted another set of standards instead, this chapter will also be useful to you. Exemplary teaching behaviors are for the most part universal. Therefore, the set of standards you have chosen will have concepts similar to the InTASC core standards and, in some cases, similar wording. For example, standards offered by the NBPTS for early childhood teachers contain a standard called "Understanding Young Children," which targets the concept of gaining and applying knowledge of child development. It is essentially the same concept as InTASC Core Standard One "Learner Development." Because Standard One is described and depicted in this chapter, you will want to read that section carefully to gain insights into that area of teaching. Do this for all the standards in your set of goals. You can refer to Figure 1.1 in Chapter 1 and compare your standard statements to the InTASC core standards. Then return to this chapter and read the examples that apply to your teaching situation. Although the scenarios may not portray actual experiences you have had, they will help you picture opportunities for documenting your professional growth.

HOW THIS CHAPTER IS ORGANIZED

Chapter 4 is organized in the following manner:

1. ***Statement of the Standard*** In turn, each of the ten core standards or principles for effective teaching as stated by InTASC is presented.
2. ***Explanation of the Standard*** A short explanation of the standard is provided to add clarity. If you are not using InTASC core standards, this explanation of each standard will help you determine similarities and differences between your chosen goals and the ones described here.
3. ***Teaching Scenario*** Examples typical of preservice and inservice teachers' activities both inside and outside college classrooms are presented, with examples from four levels of teaching: early childhood, elementary, middle school, and secondary. The scenarios illustrate situations in which professional activities are indicators of achievement of the standards. Such illustrations will help you relate your set of standards, whether from InTASC or another source, to your everyday experiences as a preservice teacher.
4. ***Sample Rationale Pages for Artifacts.*** Following each scenario is a sample rationale page for artifacts that could document achieved competence in a particular standard. Writing rationale statements is typically the most difficult part of your portfolio development, so you will want to pay close attention to them. You may want to use the sample rationale statements in this text as models for your portfolio's rationale statements. Therefore, all sample rationale pages in this text have been identified by shading and an icon.

Remember, all of the material presented in this chapter is for the purpose of example and is not meant to imply that there is a single correct way to teach or document professional growth in a portfolio.

LEARNER DEVELOPMENT

Standard One

The teacher understands how learners grow and develop, recognizing that patterns of learning and development vary individually within and across the cognitive, linguistic, social, emotional, and physical areas, and designs and implements developmentally appropriate and challenging learning experiences.

Explanation of the Standard

A teacher working with a particular group of learners quickly realizes how each individual is unique. Even learners of approximately the same age may display vastly different developmental characteristics. Yet, in spite of wide differences, common characteristics unite learners within an age group. Although learners grow and develop at different rates and with varied abilities, there are predictable patterns and sequences to their development.

Understanding these patterns, sequences, and stages of development is essential groundwork for a teacher making instructional decisions. Educational practice, to be effective, must be rooted in the rapidly advancing research and theory of human development and learning. Often such theory cannot be translated directly into teaching practice. However, when the teacher has a broad understanding of learning and development, this knowledge can be useful in making logical hypotheses in how best to understand and thus respond to an individual or group of learners.

When teachers understand how learning occurs and how a learner's development impacts the acquisition of knowledge and skills, they are able to design and implement developmentally appropriate instruction to build on the learner's strengths and needs. Instructional decisions, however, should not be made in a vacuum. Teachers must reach out to and collaborate with other professionals, family, and community members to gather data and information in regards to a learner's developmental level. Only with this knowledge can effective and successful instruction be planned and delivered.

Teachers must carefully observe the responses of learners and the effects of their curricular choices. Rather than "covering material," teachers must evaluate the quality of the understanding of the content and the developmental appropriateness for the instructional strategies used. Thus, teachers gain knowledge from two sources about learning and development: the fields of human development and psychology, and their own observations of learners and reflections about their teaching. The following scenario depicts how a preservice teacher uses a study of Piaget's theory of child development to demonstrate her competence in "Learner Development."

Teaching Scenario

Stacey is a sophomore elementary education major. As part of the general education requirement, Stacey is taking a course in educational psychology. The works of many psychologists and learning theorists (e.g., David Ausubel, Benjamin Bloom, Lawrence Kohlberg, Jean Piaget, Erik Erikson) are dealt with in class. Stacey must research one learning theorist, write a paper on his work, and use that knowledge to assess a learner's developmental level. Stacey selects Jean Piaget and his work on cognitive development as the subject for her project.

In the paper portion of her project, Stacey presents background information on Piaget. She reports on his early studies in biology and how he became interested in child development. She discusses the principal concepts of Piaget's theory: schemata, assimilation, accommodation, and equilibration. The bulk of the paper, however, discusses Piaget's four stages of cognitive development: sensorimotor, preoperational, concrete operational, and formal operational. She states that Piaget believed that all learners pass through these stages in order and that no learner can skip a stage, although different learners pass through the stages at somewhat different rates.

Stacey selects Piaget's theory of conservation for the application portion of her project. This principle states that the properties of objects—such as mass, volume, and number—remain the same, despite changes in the form of the objects. She asks for and receives permission to work with a nine-year-old neighbor. Stacey wants to determine whether her neighbor possesses conservation of mass reasoning. She replicates Piaget's classic experiment using beakers containing colored liquid. Looking at two beakers of equal size that contain the same amount of liquid, Stacey's neighbor states that the amount of liquid in the containers is the same. After watching Stacey pour the liquid from one beaker to a third taller and thinner beaker, her neighbor is still able to state that the beakers contain similar amounts of liquid. Stacey concludes that the child does, indeed, possess conservation of mass reasoning and infers that her neighbor is at Piaget's concrete operational stage.

In the conclusion of her paper, Stacey discusses the relationship between knowledge of Piaget's stages of cognitive development and effective instruction. Knowing the cognitive levels of learners makes it possible for a teacher to plan, design, and deliver challenging and appropriate learning experiences.

Stacey's professor returns the project with favorable comments. The professor is impressed with Stacey's research, writing skills, and ability to relate Piaget's theory to instructional practice. She feels the project indicates Stacey has a sound understanding of both Piaget's work and his contributions to education. Because of her interest in the subject and the professor's positive evaluation, Stacey decides to include the project in her portfolio. Her rationale page is shown here.

SAMPLE RATIONALE PAGE

Artifact for Standard One: Learner Development
Name of Artifact: Project on Piaget and Cognitive Development
Date: October 23, 2012
Course: PSY 208—Educational Psychology
Rationale:

   To document my knowledge of learner development, I have selected a project I completed for an educational psychology course. The project focused on Jean Piaget and his work in cognitive development. In addition, I used the knowledge gained through my research to determine the cognitive level of a nine-year-old girl. I described the four stages of cognitive development and common tasks learners at each stage can accomplish. I then replicated Piaget's classic experiment dealing with conservation of mass. Based upon the results of the experiment, I determined the girl was working at the concrete operational stage. I concluded my project by discussing how knowledge of Piaget's work can positively impact instructional decisions and learning experiences. I have also included with this paper the positive comments my professor made concerning my work. The research I conducted for this paper and my ability to relate Piaget's work to classroom practice demonstrate my knowledge of learner development. Piaget's work has greatly influenced my outlook on child development. As I provide learning opportunities for students in my future classes, I will continue to observe my students closely and reflect Piagetian principles in my teaching.

LEARNING DIFFERENCES

Standard Two

The teacher uses understanding of individual differences and diverse cultures and communities to ensure inclusive learning environments that enable each learner to meet high standards.

Explanation of the Standard

Learners enter the classroom with a broad spectrum of learning differences, abilities, and skills. These differences range from learning disabilities to giftedness and include unique learning styles, diverse cultural backgrounds, and exceptional needs. The skillful teacher understands that learners possess a range of abilities that are based upon their individual experiences, skill development, talents, prior learning, social interactions, languages, cultures, and family and community values. Given this wide spectrum of differences, the role of the teacher is to assess each learner's developmental levels and abilities in all areas and align the learning environments and experiences to best accommodate the learner's needs. To master this role, a teacher must be a disciplined observer of learning and behavior and understand how to use data to diagnose, guide, and instruct. Furthermore, the teacher must design instruction that maximizes learners' strengths and supports their academic achievement. As a result, learners in these classrooms are valued for their uniqueness and encouraged to respect the individual differences of others.

Accomplished teachers understand the need to adapt instruction to meet the diverse needs of each learner. There are multiple strategies teachers can employ to accommodate learners, such as redesigning task assignments, adjusting time for completion of activities, using technology to enhance learning and the curriculum, providing multisensory resources, organizing peer tutoring, and designing learning activities that honor cultural differences.

These accomplished teachers will also collaborate with other professionals to foster an inclusive learning environment for all learners. They participate in the development of individualized education plans and family-centered assessments for learners with special developmental and learning needs.

The following scenario depicts how a preservice student teacher worked with professionals and families to assist learners with learning disabilities and a gifted learner to meet the standards of their social studies curriculum and address their individual education plans.

Teaching Scenario

Rosa is a preservice student teacher in Ms. Jones' sixth-grade departmentalized social studies class. As part of the university requirements, she schedules a meeting with Ms. Jones two weeks before the beginning of the school year to discuss her upcoming placement and to review Ms. Jones' expectations. During their meeting, Rosa is told that there are three learners with learning disabilities and one learner with a gifted individualized education plan (IEP) enrolled in the class in which she will be teaching her unit on local history. During her first week at the school, Rosa studies the IEPs for the four identified learners and reflects upon strategies she could use throughout the unit to address each learner's needs and meet the academic standards for social studies.

Each learner in the class is assigned a research topic about the local community. Rosa schedules individual conferences with each learner to discuss his or her topic and to help the learners outline the reports. Rosa extends her conference times for learners with learning disabilities and offers each student various formats for outlining and a list of references to help them organize their projects. In accordance with the learners' IEPs, she communicates with the parents of each learner and discusses ways the parents could assist the learners at home. She also meets with the gifted learner, the teacher of gifted education, and her own cooperating teacher to develop an addendum to the assignment that would provide enrichment through extended research and reporting. Throughout the two-week unit, Rosa provides additional time to meet with the identified learners and provides opportunities for peer tutoring during class discussions.

Rosa decides to include this experience in her portfolio for Standard Two. She includes a copy of the conference schedules and the checklist she developed to document the additional strategies she used to assist these learners. She includes anecdotal notes from each learner's conference and communications with parents. She also includes a copy of the outlines written by the learners and a copy of the plans for the addendum designed for the gifted learner. She includes a rationale page, similar to the following example, to justify how her work addresses Standard Two.

SAMPLE RATIONALE PAGE

Artifact for Standard Two: Learning Differences
Name of Artifact: Social Studies Local History Project
Date: September 18, 2012
Course: EDE 461—Student Teaching
Rationale:

During my student teaching experience, I had a wonderful class of sixth graders that included three learners with learning disabilities and one with a gifted IEP. To ensure these learners could successfully complete the required project and meet the IEP requirements, I needed to adapt my instruction and the curriculum. I developed a plan to allow extra conference time and additional resources for the learners with learning disabilities. I also collaborated with their parents to discuss ways they could assist their child at home. I collaborated with the teacher of gifted education to develop an addendum for enrichment that included extended research and reporting about the community and local history. I maintained anecdotal notes during the conferences, designed a checklist to document strategies I used to assist these learners, and monitored learners' outlines. I have included examples of each artifact as evidence of my work. Each learner was successful in completion of his or her project, and the gifted learner published her paper in the school newspaper.

I believe these documents illustrate my ability to create a learning experience that meets the special needs of learners with learning disabilities and also to create an enrichment experience for a gifted learner. I recognized that my plans for the general class did not address the needs of these learners or meet the requirements of their individual education plans. I chose to design accommodations so that each learner could reach his or her potential and successfully master the project. Working with these four learners reinforced my belief that teachers must acquire a repertoire of strategies that meet the diverse needs of all learners across the learning continuum. I believe I will teach differently as a result of this experience because I understand that I must continually assess my learners and provide appropriate environments for all.

LEARNING ENVIRONMENTS

Standard Three

The teacher works with others to create environments that support individual and collaborative learning and that encourage positive social interaction, active engagement in learning, and self-motivation.

Explanation of the Standard

Effective teachers work in many ways to build positive learning environments. This task is most successful when carried out cooperatively with parents, caregivers, colleagues, and the learners themselves. Effective teachers recognize that involving students in this endeavor not only promotes growth in personal and social responsibility but also enhances the development of democratic and social values. Group rapport is enhanced as students and teachers work cooperatively to establish shared values and expectations. Teaching and modeling effective problem-solving techniques, such as conflict resolution, provides motivation for learning, positive social interaction among learners, and positive self-esteem for all. Thus, the effective teacher strives to create a learning community that fosters group decision making, collaboration, individual responsibility, and self-directed learning.

Teachers interested in building and sustaining a positive learning environment are aware of the range of behavioral phenomena confronting them. They recognize that there will be situations in which some learners are unable or unwilling to function within the parameters established by the group. In these instances, teachers must rely upon their knowledge of the principles and strategies of behavior management and issues related to all aspects of motivation. As reflective practitioners, teachers use this knowledge of theory, along with their classroom experiences, to construct ever-evolving student motivation and management strategies specific enough to guide classroom actions, yet flexible enough to accommodate the individual needs of students. Therefore, effective classroom managers understand the need to be able to define problems, identify alternatives, choose a course of action, plan for implementation, and consider the possible consequences of a given action.

Much of motivating learners and managing learning environments is about sending and receiving messages using effective interpersonal skills. Carefully planned and skillfully delivered respectful messages can issue invitations to students that school is a place to share ideas, investigate, create, and collaborate with others. School can be a place to be understood as well as a place to gain understanding. But without intentional considerations and planning, the messages actually received by the students can be conflicting, confusing, or discouraging. For this reason, teachers need to monitor their personal verbal and nonverbal communication so it is characterized by clarity, organization, enthusiasm, and sensitivity. Effective teachers consistently use active listening skills as well.

Environments and resources, as well as people, send messages. The physical environment of a classroom can communicate many things to students. For example, bright, cheerful, colorful environments are likely to set expectations that this is a happy, interesting place to be. Classrooms where all learners have work displayed are likely to communicate that everyone shares this environment and that all are valued. When frequently used materials are stored so they are easily accessible, students learn that they can be independent in this classroom. The condition and organization of materials also communicate the importance the teacher attaches to the work that is done with those materials.

Part of the effective teacher's role, therefore, is to select, adapt, and create a physical environment and a broad range of instructional resources that engage the students in exciting learning and that send the messages intended.

The following teaching scenario shows how a preservice teacher assessed his ability to create a positive learning environment and modified his own teaching behaviors to improve the climate of his classroom.

Teaching Scenario

While enrolled in an early field experience class, Mikhail has the opportunity to spend a few hours every week in a daycare classroom working with children ages three to five. Mikhail soon realizes that these young children can be very impetuous and need a great deal of support from teachers in developing self-control and learning how to function in a group.

The college instructor in the class addresses promoting positive guidance as one of her seminar topics. In class, Mikhail and his classmates practice phrasing requests and directions to young children in a positive, encouraging way that would invite the children's cooperation and teach them problem-solving and negotiating skills. Mikhail values this instruction a great deal because he realizes that he has a tendency to be directive and often negative with children, using a great many *don't*s. Mikhail decides to systematically practice these positive guidance techniques in the classroom with children.

He asks a fellow classmate who is doing field work with him at the daycare center to observe and record any negative, discouraging, or demanding comments that he makes to the children. After receiving her observations, Mikhail reflects with his fellow classmate and his field site supervisor on how he could have communicated those same requests to the children in a positive, encouraging way. Gradually, Mikhail finds he is gaining in his ability to spontaneously use positive verbal guidance. He is also becoming more likely to invite problem solving rather than solve problems through correcting children.

Mikhail is proud of this growth; he can see how his behavior is resulting in a much better rapport with these children and is helping to create a more positive social climate. Mikhail decides to document this work. He includes in his portfolio a video recording of his interactions with the group, anecdotal records of his growth based on the observations of his classmate, and the following rationale page.

SAMPLE RATIONALE PAGE

Artifact for Standard Three: Learning Environments
Name of Artifact: Evidence of Positive Verbal Guidance
Date: March 4, 2011
Course: ECE 203—Field Experiences with Young Children
Rationale:

I have chosen to use two documents that indicate the growth I have attained in understanding how to create a positive learning environment with very young children. The first is a set of anecdotal records of interactions I had in a classroom of three- to five-year-olds and my reflections on the outcomes of those interactions. The anecdotal records show growth in my ability to formulate positive, encouraging requests and responses to children. The second is a video recording of me near the end of the field experience; it shows informal conversations with children and a teacher-directed activity. In this recording, I demonstrate my ability to gain children's cooperation by the way I speak with them. I also demonstrate how I help the children solve problems with their peers, encouraging cooperation rather than taking over the situation. The strategies I am employing lead to positive social interaction and positive individual and group motivation. I am particularly proud of my professional growth as a result of this experience. I had never before realized the importance of phrasing requests and directions in a positive manner. My ability to motivate children and manage my future classroom has been greatly enhanced.

CONTENT KNOWLEDGE

Standard Four

The teacher understands the central concepts, tools of inquiry, and structures of the discipline(s) he or she teaches and creates learning experiences that make these aspects of the discipline accessible and meaningful for learners to assure mastery of the content.

Explanation of the Standard

Content knowledge is universally considered an essential attribute for effective teaching and successful learning. The most meaningful and lasting learning occurs when individual learners construct knowledge, rather than memorizing it from a textbook. The role of the teacher is to help learners build their own knowledge through acting on materials and engaging in meaningful experiences. To create these experiences, teachers must possess an in-depth understanding of the central concepts, assumptions, debates, tools of inquiry, and ways of knowing that are central to the disciplines they teach.

Content knowledge also requires an understanding of inquiry used in various disciplines. Teachers need to engage learners in applying investigative methods found in the discipline being taught. When historians seek to learn about an event in American history, they search for multiple and varied primary sources. Diaries, photographs, maps, and government records are studied, questioned, and analyzed. Employing the same methodology used by scholars allows social studies/history teachers to engage learners in generating knowledge and testing hypotheses according to the methods of inquiry and standards of evidence used in the discipline.

In every classroom, it is critical that teachers evaluate resources and curriculum materials for their comprehensiveness, accuracy, and usefulness for representing particular ideas and concepts in the discipline. Appropriate state content standards must also be identified when selecting materials and designing learning experiences for learners. In-depth content knowledge is essential for the identification of both appropriate curriculum materials and state standards.

The following scenario describes how a teacher education student integrates his knowledge of American history and the tools used by historians to develop and teach a unit of study on the Oregon Trail.

Teaching Scenario

Charlie, a middle school social studies methods preservice teacher, is assigned to teach eighth graders about the Oregon Trail. He begins his work by reviewing how the topic is dealt with in a traditional social studies curriculum. He examines several eighth-grade social studies texts and finds that the Oregon Trail experience is covered very briefly. Charlie is also dissatisfied with the manner in which the subject is treated: primarily through names, dates, and facts. Charlie would like his learners to gain an understanding and appreciation of what the four-month journey was like for those individuals and families who made the long and dangerous trip. He also wishes to teach and have his learners use the same methods employed by historians when they study an event in United States history.

Charlie learned from his professor that, according to the research, learners benefit most from forms of narrative history that involve the particular—that is, how a person or small group copes with a particular problem in a particular place at a particular time and under a particular set of circumstances. This type of historical material is most commonly found in original source materials such as journals, diaries, letters, biographies, and historical fiction.

Knowing that historians always attempt to locate and analyze multiple sources to learn about an event, Charlie decides to focus his instruction around several diaries written by young people during the overland crossing. The social studies textbook, rather than being the primary source of information, will become one of many secondary resource materials. Charlie supplements the diaries with archival photographs from which he hopes his students will gain further understanding and appreciation for the overland experience.

The lessons are designed so that Charlie's learners travel the Oregon Trail along with the diary authors. They read of the daily routine, the blazing heat, the lack of water, the river crossings, contact with Native Americans, and so forth. Charlie's learners can share the joy of those who successfully reach Oregon and the grief of those who lose loved ones on the trail.

Charlie lists the major concepts that he will address, locates appropriate state content standards, designs corresponding instructional activities, and lists necessary materials. He plans to begin instruction by identifying and assessing his learners' prior knowledge of the content and to culminate the unit by having learners write an imaginary diary as if they were crossing the Oregon Trail.

Charlie is pleased with the finished product. The instructor is also pleased; Charlie receives favorable comments. Charlie decides his Oregon Trail unit of study would be an excellent choice to include in his portfolio.

SAMPLE RATIONALE PAGE

Artifact for Standard Four: Content Knowledge
Name of Artifact: Oregon Trail Teaching Plans
Date: October 2, 2012
Course: EDE 306—Teaching Social Studies in the Middle School
Rationale:
　　I have included this set of lessons in my portfolio to document my content knowledge. The topic, the Oregon Trail, is primarily dealt with through the use of a number of diaries written by overland pioneers. Current research on how children best learn history indicates that using a primary source document such as a diary would be a particularly effective technique because learners best relate to historical events through some kind of narrative. Learning about the Oregon Trail experience through the words of someone close to their own age would be interesting and enjoyable for my students. These lessons are historically accurate and are constructed in agreement with the current research on how to effectively teach history to children. I believe they document my content knowledge. From this experience, I have learned the importance of knowing the subject matter that I teach. In particular, I learned how to use primary source documents when teaching about historical events. My future lesson plans for social studies will include the use of such resources.

APPLICATION OF CONTENT

Standard Five

The teacher understands how to connect concepts and use differing perspectives to engage learners in critical thinking, creativity, and collaborative problem solving related to authentic local and global issues.

Explanation of the Standard

Learners in the twenty-first century need the ability to apply content to real-world challenges and situations and to address meaningful issues by using the prerequisite high-order skills and rigorous content knowledge. They need to grow in their ability to view issues from multiple perspectives in order to understand issues deeply. As learners have opportunities to apply what they know, they find that content becomes much more relevant. Teachers need to be able to design curriculum that gives learners opportunities to apply content and to view the world through multiple lenses.

In the past when educators built curriculum, they typically used a "take apart and simplify" approach; that is, they separated complex understandings and abilities into disciplines, subjects, and sequenced units of study. Often the units were further organized so that the simplest ideas were presented first as the building blocks for more sophisticated understanding.

While this may seem like a logical approach to curriculum building, it has its limitations. An approach that keeps things applicable and connected is much more likely to promote cross-disciplinary skills such as problem solving, use of technology, collaboration, and critical thinking. The challenges for learners presented by a "connected curriculum" promote creativity and innovation. Learners achieve in-depth understanding of content while simultaneously developing higher-level thinking skills, communication skills, and positive dispositions toward learning as they actively strive to make sense out of their world. The "take apart" approach to curriculum has its place, but an effective teacher must be equally skilled at creating and implementing more complex and connected learning opportunities.

Curriculum that connects concepts and uses different perspectives takes various forms including interdisciplinary thematic and multidisciplinary studies, and problem- and project-based learning. These options differ in their driving force (for example, a theme, a common topic, a project, or a problem). All of these approaches put the teacher more in the role of facilitator, tutor, supporter, and coach rather than instructor. The teacher is often a colearner in these approaches as he or she becomes comfortable with moving outside his or her own discipline to pursue connections. In these approaches learners are given a degree of control over goals and lines of inquiry.

Integrated curriculum options have other things in common. All these approaches cross disciplinary lines when it is natural to do so. Learning starts with complex tasks or issues while staying connected and whole throughout. Curriculum uses authentic activities with tasks that are as close to "real world" as possible. Multiple resources and tools are used. Learners are actively involved in searching for meaning. Often the learning is developed collaboratively in small groups. The teacher works to guarantee that, when appropriate, multiple social and cultural perspectives are brought to bear on the investigations.

It is important that educators not regard integrated curriculum options as an "add on" to the district or state curriculum. While it might be interesting to pursue problems, themes, or projects unrelated to curriculum outcomes, it is generally not advisable to do so. Time is short, and the mandated curriculum is full. Therefore, teachers should design studies involving problems, projects, and themes as a way of addressing state and district learner indicators and benchmarks. In fact, because of the integration of disciplines, teachers often find that these approaches are an effective way to cope with the explosion of information and a crowded curriculum.

Teaching Scenario

Madison is beginning her first teaching assignment; she is excited to learn that environmental studies is part of the district curriculum for sixth grade. She is interested in developing an interdisciplinary theme study for her sixth graders on caring for the environment. However, as Madison is developing her thematic unit, she makes an interesting discovery: Her school is not modeling part of what she wants to teach: There is no recycling effort in her school.

Madison changes direction slightly, moving from a theme study to a project-based study. With the support of her principal, she engages her sixth graders in working on a project to initiate a recycling program in their school. They research the advantages of recycling, the community resources available to help with recycling, and the difficulties and challenges to the school, including the costs. Furthermore, they research how to prepare a proposal for change and how to advocate for change.

The learners work in small groups to develop a plan for their school. Once the students negotiate a class plan, they present it to the principal as well as to some staff and teachers in the school. These professionals offer feedback and suggestions to the students. Based on this feedback, the class revises the plan. Once their plan is approved, the principal and Madison help the learners reach out to the community in order to obtain the materials and resources needed to implement the plan. When all is in place, teams of sixth graders visit every class in the school to win support for this effort.

Madison is eager to document this exciting experience in her portfolio under the standard Application of Content.

SAMPLE RATIONALE PAGE

Artifact for Standard Five: Application of Content
Name of Artifact: Project-Based Learning Experience
Date: May 10, 2013
Rationale:

   I have decided to document a very successful project-based learning experience with my sixth graders. The driving force for their investigations was the project of creating a workable school-wide recycling program. The learners were successful at analyzing the complexities of recycling and were creative in developing a plan tailored to the needs and realities of their school. As they worked on this project, they refined several communication skills, especially reading in the content area and speaking persuasively, and met several district goals in environmental science and social studies. Their written plan serves as my documentation for my growth in the ability to connect concepts and integrate goals from various disciplines. In the future I will look for more opportunities to create meaningful integrated learning opportunities. I have filed this document under Standard Five because the most important thing I gained while guiding this learning experience was how to connect concepts and facilitate critical thinking skills in learners as they applied content.

ASSESSMENT

Standard Six

The teacher understands and uses multiple methods of assessment to engage learners in their own growth, to monitor learner progress, and to guide the teacher's and learner's decision making.

Explanation of Standard

The purpose of assessment is to assist learners, teachers, schools, parents, and caregivers in recognizing what students have learned and to identify areas in which they need improvement. Teachers gather, synthesize, and evaluate many different types of information about their learners to make effective decisions about instruction.

Traditional assessment has been based on specific information that teachers acquire. Observations, tests on content, and standardized tests are examples of traditional evaluative measures that provide indicators that suggest learning has taken place. These traditional measures may tell little, however, about the depth of knowledge in relation to solving real-life problems. New approaches to assessment have tried to address this need by focusing on performance samples in which learners demonstrate that they can perform a task, such as giving a speech, playing an instrument, or writing a story. Some of these tasks are called *alternative assessments* because they take place in a contrived context. They are an improvised or created "alternative" to a real-life problem-solving situation. In contrast, other performance tasks are authentic assessments because learners demonstrate learning in a real-life setting. For example, a learner might be asked to give a speech while running for school office. If the learner wants to be elected, the speech must be convincing enough to accomplish this. This type of authentic assessment measures not only the learner's ability to effectively demonstrate skills or solve problems but also his or her ability to assume responsibility for directing his or her own learning. Because of the benefits of using a variety of assessment strategies, many teachers assist learners with organizing their work samples into portfolios. This approach to assessment relies on work samples and performance tasks that reflect the academic growth of the learner over time. A learner portfolio should include a variety of both authentic and alternative assessment samples.

It is also important for the teacher to balance the use of formative and summative assessments. Formative assessments take place while learning progresses: The teacher observes, makes notes, and monitors learner responses during lessons, to make sure that each learner is meeting objectives and demonstrating understanding before moving on to more difficult tasks. Such assessments are ongoing and may involve learning logs, journals, observations, anecdotal notes, and checklists while learners complete tasks during lessons. Summative assessments are made after a lesson, unit, or topic of study is complete. These assessments are usually quantitative but can take many forms as teachers realize the importance of providing learners with multiple ways of demonstrating their knowledge and skill. Teachers use both summative and formative assessments to inform their teaching and can give learners appropriate and effective feedback that guides their progress.

The following scenario shows how a preservice field experience student from the university and a cooperating teacher gather, synthesize, and evaluate different types of assessment information in order to direct instruction.

Teaching Scenario

Emma is an education major enrolled in a reading methods class. The field component of this course requires her to plan a reading lesson and teach it to a small group of learners in third grade.

At first, Emma observes the teacher and learners and their interaction during reading lessons. She takes notes on learners' reactions to the lesson and lists ideas that she has for facilitating their understanding while they read and for checking their comprehension after they are finished reading. She makes plans for teaching a reading lesson using the children's book, *Hey, Al,* by Arthur Yorinks. She plans to teach her learners how to infer the theme of this Caldecott award-winning book.

On the day of the lesson, Emma is excited because she has planned activities that will facilitate her learners' understanding of the story before, during, and after their reading. She has also planned for formative assessments during the reading process so that she can adjust her teaching accordingly. Before they read, she assesses the learners' knowledge of important vocabulary in the book by giving them a large cutout of a stoplight and several word cards. They talk with their partners about the words and then place the cards on the colors of the stoplight— green indicates that they know the words, yellow means they are unsure of the words, and red means that they definitely do not know the words. This formative, learner-oriented assessment engages her learners in their own assessments and gives her vocabulary instruction more efficacy. During reading, she asks learners to stop at places in the book and discuss predictions and inferences; she makes notes on a checklist that record the quality of her learners' responses to questions as they read and helps her make plans for future strategy lessons. After her learners finish reading, Emma asks them to create an illustrated and written retelling of the story, and explain how its theme reminds them of a personal experience. She uses a rubric that she has prepared to assess her learners' ability to name the story elements as well as their personal connections to the theme. After comparing her learners' work to the rubric, she determines that all of them can identify story elements quite well, but three of them have difficulty making personal connections to the theme of the story. Thus, she makes plans to teach a strategy lesson on inferring to this small group of learners.

Emma is pleased that she has had the opportunity to observe and participate in this reading assessment project. She has collected all of her learners' work samples as well as her rubrics, checklists, and notes. With the permission of the cooperating teacher and the learners, all of these samples go into Emma's portfolio. She is careful to delete the learners' names and other forms of identification.

SAMPLE RATIONALE PAGE

Artifact for Standard Six: Assessment
Name of Artifact: Assessments in a Guided Reading Lesson
Date: January 26, 2012
Course: ELE 301—Reading Methods, Assessments, and Interventions
Rationale:

I placed my lesson plan for a guided reading lesson under Standard Six, Assessment. For this project, I created and taught a reading lesson for third grade learners, using the book *Hey, Al* by Arthur Yorinks. This reading lesson demonstrates my ability to assess learners' work as they learn how to make inferences when reading.

To begin the project, I observed Mrs. Wright, my cooperating teacher, and her learners as she taught guided reading lessons. While observing, I took notes on learners' responses to questions during and after their reading. Based on my observations, Mrs. Wright and I determined that these third-grade learners needed some additional instruction in making inferences as they read. I developed some plans for facilitating their understanding of the author's implied messages while they read and for checking their comprehension of inferences after they finish reading. We decided that I would teach a guided reading lesson using the children's book *Hey, Al* by Arthur Yorinks.

My lesson included before, during, and after reading activities that focused on implied messages in text and facilitated my learners' understandings of the author's theme. Before they read, I assessed the learners' knowledge of important vocabulary in the book using a self-selected activity that enabled them to show me how much they already knew about the words. I also used formative assessments during the reading process, in which I asked learners to stop at places in the book and discuss predictions and inferences. These formative assessments gave me an idea of how well learners were making inferences while reading. After reading, I asked learners to illustrate and write a retelling of the story that included their explanation of how the author's theme reminded them of a personal experience. I created and implemented a rubric that assessed my learners' ability to name the story elements, as well as their connections to the theme. My analysis of the learners' assessments indicated that all of the learners were able to identify story elements quite well, but three of them had difficulty making personal connections to the theme of the story. This summative assessment enabled me to make plans to teach a strategy lesson on inferring to this small group of learners. All of the learners' work samples, my rubrics, checklists, and notes are included as artifacts for this standard.

I have gained much valuable experience in using informal assessments to determine my learners' strengths and needs. When I teach lessons of this nature in the future, I will be able to use and adapt the assessment instruments that I created and use these experiences to inform my decision making.

PLANNING FOR INSTRUCTION

Standard Seven

The teacher plans instruction that supports every student in meeting rigorous learning goals by drawing upon knowledge of content areas, curriculum, cross-disciplinary skills, and pedagogy, as well as knowledge of learners and the community context.

Explanation of the Standard

An effective teacher plans learning experiences based on a set of diverse factors, each of which influences the learning outcome. First, the subject matter is considered. It is important that the teacher have a thorough knowledge of the subject being taught as well as an understanding of teaching strategies and learning experiences that are unique to that subject. Second, the individual needs of learners are of utmost importance. Teachers need to be able to create short- and long-term plans that are linked to learner needs based on formative and summative assessment data, information gained from working collaboratively with professionals who have specialized expertise, and knowledge of learners' background experiences and interests. The effective teacher plans well and yet is ready to respond to unanticipated classroom events and adapt those plans to ensure learner progress and motivation. Third, the teacher is well versed in a variety of evidence-based instructional strategies, using multiple resources and technological tools, and makes plans for using them to effectively meet learners' needs. Finally, as public educators, teachers need to be sensitive to the input of the community when making instructional plans. Community input can take shape in the form of curriculum goals adopted by the school district, as well as national and state standards.

All of these considerations are tempered by the teacher's ability and willingness to adjust and revise plans according to learners' needs and interests, as well as unforeseen circumstances. Thus, as teachers engage in both long- and short-term planning, they must be flexible enough to consider these contexts: subject matter, state standards, local school district goals, current educational issues, legal issues, family and community considerations, public policies, and community resources. Tying all these together are the interests, needs, and aptitudes of each of the learners being taught. While in the classroom, teachers need to be reflective of their current practice and open to adjustments and revisions that become necessary in working with a diverse group of learners. This self-reflection is evident in the teaching scenario that follows.

Teaching Scenario

Juanita, a newly tenured sixth-grade teacher in an urban school, is in the process of updating her teaching portfolio. In searching for examples to document this standard, she reflects on lessons that demonstrate how she addressed the diverse needs of learners through school curriculum goals and community-based resources. She chooses a set of lesson plans that describe lessons in which she incorporates authentic learning experiences to teach her learners how to use persuasive language.

Juanita begins the first lesson by showing her learners two breakfast cereals—one was a chocolate-flavored cereal with a brightly colored box that contained a prize inside, and the other was a granola-based cereal usually marketed to adults. She asks the learners, "Which cereal would you prefer to eat for breakfast? Let's vote." She passes out slips of paper for them to write their preference and then tallies the votes. A large majority prefers the sugary cereal, and the students verify this result by creating a bar graph. She asks the learners to discuss with a partner their reasons for choosing the chocolate cereal and asks them to share these ideas with the whole group. As they share, she lists the reasons on the white board. Then she announces, "Ok, I have a challenge for you. We've listed many reasons that you prefer this chocolate-flavored cereal. But here's a problematic situation for you. Assume that you are the marketing director for the company that makes the less popular cereal. Your job is to increase sales of this cereal and convince consumers that the nutritious cereal is just as good as the chocolate-flavored one. Your 'consumers' will be the fourth-grade class down the hall. You'll need to create an advertisement using persuasive language. You may present your ad in one of the following forms: video, glog, audio podcast, photographic essay, blog, or poster."

Throughout the week, learners read examples of loaded words in books and advertisements and create lists of such words, analyze magazine ads to determine their effectiveness, and view commercials that Juanita had downloaded to study their persuasiveness. They also do some research on the cereal that they are attempting to sell—its nutritional content, appearance, and packaging. Finally, they survey the learners in the fourth-grade class to determine their interests and eating habits. Armed with this information, they work in small groups to design advertisements intended to convince ten-year-olds to eat a more nutritious cereal.

These inquiries lead to additional explorations of persuasive language. Juanita extends her students' learning across disciplines as the class completes their project and embarks on other explorations of persuasive language, including examining propaganda in political ads, loaded words in speeches, and possible biases in newspaper and Internet articles.

In all of these lessons, mathematical standards are addressed through the learners' bar graphs. Science standards are met as they use scientific inquiry to determine the problem and develop a hypothesis for changing the eating habits of children. Language arts and reading standards are met as they use critical reading and thoughtful literacy skills to analyze the use of persuasive language in several forms of media. And finally, technology standards are addressed as learners prepare their advertisements in response to the problematic situation. Juanita uses many community resources to help teach her lessons, including school and local librarians, a marketing director for a local building supply company, a local newspaper journalist, and even a campaign manager for a local politician.

To culminate these learning experiences, learners share their advertisements with the fourth-grade class, collect data, and report the results.

SAMPLE RATIONALE PAGE

Artifact for Standard Seven: Instructional Planning Skills
Name of Artifact: Series of Lessons on Use of Persuasive Language
Date: April 12, 2012
Rationale:

The artifact I chose to use in documenting my instructional planning skills is a set of plans that I wrote and implemented, in which I taught my sixth-grade learners how to use persuasive language in an authentic advertisement. Their goal was to create an advertisement, persuading fourth-graders that a healthy cereal was just as delicious and enjoyable as a sugary cereal. I have included the goals and objectives, an outline of the daily lesson plans, samples of learners' original advertisements, data collection charts, and rubrics that assessed their work. These lessons integrated the subject areas of mathematics, science, social studies, language arts, and consumer science, all woven together through the use of technology.

I filed this unit plan under Standard Seven because it clearly demonstrates my ability to plan, deliver, and adjust instruction based on the knowledge of subject, learners, community, and curriculum goals. Learners were actively engaged in solving a real-life problem—that of using persuasive language in an advertisement for a product that is usually considered a "hard sell" for their audience, fourth-grade children. My lessons include the introduction to the problem, in which my class identified their favorite cereal and realized through data collection and analysis that they preferred the chocolate-flavored one. Subsequent lessons included all of the activities that they needed to complete in order to solve the problematic situation, in which they were given the challenge of convincing other learners to eat healthier cereals. Objectives included determining the most persuasive language, researching the nutritional content of cereals and the visual appeal of their packaging, surveying another class to determine their cereal favorites, creating an ad using an effective medium, and determining the effectiveness of the advertisement.

As I reflect upon the entire set of lessons, I believe evidence contained in the learners' research, investigations, use of persuasive language, and analysis of their own data attest to the connections learners made to the content standards. This experience has encouraged me to continue in the future to find other ways to use problematic situations that help my learners meet standards while engaging in authentic learning.

INSTRUCTIONAL STRATEGIES

Standard Eight

The teacher understands and uses a variety of instructional strategies to encourage learners to develop deep understanding of content areas and their connections, and to build skills to apply knowledge in meaningful ways.

Explanation of the Standard

Teachers deal daily with many complexities, including differences among their learners in terms of abilities, attitudes, and learning preferences. For these widely varying learners, there are multiple goals and objectives to be met, including those dealing with content, basic skills, problem solving, attitudes, dispositions, and critical-thinking skills. It is clear that no routine or "pet" teaching approach can effectively meet all of these needs. Effective teachers draw from a wide repertoire of instructional strategies and models, adjusting their choices to meet their intended objectives and the needs of particular learners.

There are many instances in which the most efficient and effective way to teach certain kinds of knowledge is through expository teaching or teacher-directed, step-by-step learning. In such cases, direct instruction, presentations, and skills practice are appropriate. However, there are many other times when methods that appear time consuming yield the greatest results in the long run. When learners are given the time and materials to be active investigators, they are able to construct a basic framework of knowledge within which to expand their understanding.

Learning for understanding often requires experimentation, problem solving, collaboration, and manipulation of physical objects. Therefore, teachers need models of teaching that include inquiry learning, cooperative learning, concept attainment, interdisciplinary learning, and class discussions. These models have as a goal the formation of cognitive structures including concepts, generalizations, dispositions, and understandings rather than simple attainment of specific facts or mastery of discrete skills. As teachers understand the wide variety of instructional strategies available, they will be better able to choose and combine them to integrate affective and cognitive development and to educate for understanding, both of content and of self. In the scenario that follows, an inservice teacher combines a promising array of strategies to meet a content goal.

Teaching Scenario

Alicia is in her second year of teaching science to ninth graders who have been targeted as students needing extra assistance. Many of her learners have learning or attention challenges. She is in the process of revising her year-long curriculum plans. Alicia wrote daily reflections during the previous year, and while rereading the reflections, she finds that many assignments and lessons worked well, while others need revision. Alicia sees a pattern. Most of the topics the learners seemed to struggle with were the more conceptual or abstract topics that are very difficult to explain. The learners had difficulty grasping topics that are not something they can see in the world around them.

One topic that emerges as needing major revision is balancing chemical equations. During Alicia's first year of teaching, she did not expect students to have difficulty with the topic because it had been so long since she learned it, and by now it was quite simple for her. Because of this, she relied solely on an oral explanation of the topic, and learners did not succeed at mastering this material. Alicia thinks hard about what best enables her learners to learn. She knows that students learn better if they have some way to see what is happening. She makes it a goal to have some concrete image for the learners for every topic in her curriculum. She knows this will be easier for some topics like force and more difficult for other topics like chemical bonding. She also realizes that learners benefit from repeated exposure to a topic, especially when different methods of communication are used each time. Alicia predicts that the repetition would benefit all learners and that some modes of communication would particularly benefit individual learners. Keeping all that she had discovered in mind, Alicia develops a series of lessons to teach balancing chemical equations using a variety of instructional strategies. In these lessons, she includes mental images, multiple communication methods, and repetition.

Alicia welcomes the opportunity to teach these revised lessons on balancing chemical equations, noting that the learners are more engaged in the content than they had been the previous year when she tried to quickly and verbally explain the topic. Alicia is pleased but not surprised when assessments on balancing chemical equations show that the learners are demonstrating much greater comprehension and retention than learners achieved the previous year. She decides to document this success in her portfolio.

SAMPLE RATIONALE PAGE

Artifact for Standard Eight: Instructional Strategies
Name of Artifact: Teacher-Made Materials on Balancing Chemical Equations
Date: December 6, 2013
Rationale:

I believe the most effective approach for all students, particularly those needing extra support, is the use of multiple instructional techniques. This is also especially important when teaching abstract concepts. For that reason, as an artifact for instructional strategies I have chosen to include a packet of teacher-made materials designed to teach the difficult topic of balancing chemical equations. These lessons were developed during my second year of teaching. The first day's lesson was a hands-on activity that proved to be especially effective for both visual and bodily kinesthetic learners. The activity materials and photos of students completing the activity are included as artifacts. The second day I combined a PowerPoint presentation with a verbal explanation of the concept. The PowerPoint uses a color-coordinated system to simplify the concept. A printout of the presentation is used as an artifact. Following the PowerPoint presentation, the students were given a practice worksheet. The worksheet is scaffolded to gradually lead the students to completing questions without assistance. It begins with a typed explanation of the concept. Then an example is done for them. Next, there are guided questions, and finally there are questions without guidance. This worksheet is also included as an artifact. The final activity was a laboratory exercise that applies the concept learned. A copy of the laboratory directions is included. This lesson plan series worked well for all types of learners and proved to be highly effective, as indicated by ongoing and final assessments. In the future, I will attempt to always engage my students through a wide variety of carefully selected and prepared instructional strategies.

PROFESSIONAL LEARNING AND ETHICAL PRACTICE

Standard Nine

The teacher engages in ongoing professional learning and uses evidence to continually evaluate his/her practice, particularly the effects of his/her choices and actions on others (learners, families, other professionals, and the community), and adapts practice to meet the needs of each learner.

Explanation of the Standard

An effective teacher is one who seeks opportunities to grow professionally from learners, colleagues, and family and community members, just as these individuals learn from the teacher. In an effort to match instruction to the needs of learners, this teacher spends much time evaluating the implications of his or her teaching decisions in the classroom. The teacher uses state and local academic standards, learner data, and best practices grounded in research as he or she aligns curriculum and instruction to meet the individual needs of the learner. This teacher crafts his or her professional development plan based upon professional feedback and learner success. This is the mark of a reflective practitioner. Such self-reflection leads to greater knowledge about the learners, the subjects being taught, and the act of teaching.

Self-reflection also takes place in considering the teacher's relationships with parents and educational professionals. The responsibilities of educators in a democratic society include working with a community of concerned individuals who rally around one central goal—educating children. Children learn much from experiences within their families and the outside world. Recognizing these facts, the teacher must cultivate strong relationships with parents and caregivers as well as with educational professionals, constantly reevaluating the effects of his or her decisions on all who are involved with the education of the learners.

This constant evaluation of choices extends itself outside the classroom. Indeed, a teaching professional is one who has a need for continuing education. Certification is only the first step in a long process of continual development as a professional. Growing professionally means learning new ways to design lesson plans, comprehending subject matter more thoroughly, managing a classroom more effectively, understanding laws related to learner rights and teacher responsibilities and applying technology to advance learning in the classroom. The teacher must also have the ability to constantly self-evaluate and act critically. New ideas, together with classroom experience, form a stronger theoretical base from which he or she works, allowing for more effective decision making in the classroom. Thus, it is crucial that teachers seek opportunities for professional growth and place new ideas within the theoretical framework that already exists in their classrooms.

The role of the reflective practitioner is demonstrated in the following scenario of Mary, a first-year elementary teacher. Note how Mary utilizes the skills of reflection and critical decision making to meet the needs of her learners and to engage in professional growth with colleagues.

Teaching Scenario

Mary, a first-year teacher, is completing her first semester at Green Valley Elementary School. One learner in her third-grade class, Michael, has been diagnosed with several emotional problems, which are affecting his academic work. While teaching this class,

Mary is constantly challenged to meet this child's needs. She monitors his academic progress as part of her electronic record keeping and maintains a daily journal entry about Michael's behavior. In this journal, she makes several entries about Michael's responses to her teaching decisions, making sure to keep his identity anonymous. She realizes that she would like to know more about how to help Michael succeed. She makes an appointment with the school psychologist, Dr. Rose, to discuss this matter. Dr. Rose makes several suggestions, which Mary also documents in her journal. Mary requests a conference with Michael's parents to share ideas and learn more about how his behavior at home may be affecting his schoolwork. His parents, impressed with her professionalism, wrote her a note praising her dedication in helping their son. In addition, Mary checks out several books on the subject of emotional disabilities in the classroom and makes note of some of the suggestions outlined. During her graduate class Ethical Teaching Practices at the university, Mary leads a discussion on this subject, based on what she has learned in her reading. She creates a handout of suggestions and shares this with her grade-level colleagues who also interact with Michael.

Mary decides to document Standard Nine with evidence of her experiences. She inserts the journal entries, the thank-you note from the parents, the bibliography of books on the subject, and the handout from the graduate class into her portfolio. Her rationale page follows.

SAMPLE RATIONALE PAGE

Artifact for Standard Nine: Professional Learning and Ethical Practice
Name of Artifact: Collection of Documents on Emotional Disabilities in School
Date: May 21, 2013
Course: EDU 410—Graduate Ethical Teaching Practices
Rationale:

My first semester teaching experience presented me with a challenge. I worked with a little boy who was experiencing emotional difficulties that prevented him from succeeding in the classroom. I felt it was important for me to learn more about what I could do to help improve his classroom experiences, so I sought additional information. I reviewed the electronic data file regarding his academic success, consulted with the school psychologist, held conferences with the parents, and read several books on the subject to add to my knowledge of how to teach this youngster and others who have his same emotional difficulties. I shared this information in a seminar discussion with my classmates and found that many of them had the same challenges. We were able to share more ideas as the discussion progressed. I gave them a handout I prepared, outlining several teaching suggestions learned from my investigation of this problem. This handout is included as documentation of this standard.

In addition, I have included my journal entries, which outline some of the questions I had about working with this child as well as some of the things I learned during my discussions with the school psychologist. I also included a thank-you note the parents wrote after our conference because it shows my commitment to building strong relationships with the family. Finally, a bibliography of books on emotional disabilities is included because it shows the research that I did to improve my knowledge of the subject. Perhaps the most important thing that I learned from this experience is that, as a teacher, I will never stop reflecting and learning. I plan to continue learning more about emotional disabilities such as those this child had; but more important, I plan to continue learning more about this profession in general.

LEADERSHIP AND COLLABORATION

Standard Ten

The teacher seeks appropriate leadership roles and opportunities to take responsibility for student learning, to collaborate with learners, families, colleagues, other school professionals, and community members to ensure learner growth, and to advance the profession.

Explanation of the Standard

Effective teachers engage in a variety of experiences within and beyond the school that promote a spirit of collaboration, collegiality, and personal growth. They work in cooperative teams, endorse collegial efforts, and seek opportunities to work with parents, caregivers, and the community at large. These teachers recognize the importance of sharing experiences and ideas.

As teachers expand their realm of interactions, they recognize how cultural identity plays an important part in the way others react to the world, how they learn, and how they view themselves. Community members and events can provide powerful examples for teachers. Effective teachers learn how to successfully use civic and community-based organizations as resources and as ways of motivating and encouraging positive growth in learners. Exposure to these influences can assist teachers in understanding the frame of reference within which the community's children operate. Connecting the school and community requires that the teacher integrate multicultural education throughout the curriculum. Teachers must be receptive to moving beyond the walls of the school and opening the door to discover the learners' other learning environments. The following scenario illustrates how Lee, a secondary mathematics education major, enhanced her learner-teaching experiences and promoted the well-being of her learners through collaboration and partnerships with colleagues, parents, and the larger community.

Teaching Scenario

Lee, a math major in secondary education, is completing her student teaching in the Springfield City School District. She enjoys the diversity she experiences among her assignments in the tenth- to twelfth-grade classrooms at Springfield High School. In addition to her teaching assignments, Lee becomes involved in an important school/community project.

During her first month at the school, she joins the afterschool tutoring team, sponsored by the Springfield Parent–Teacher Organization (PTO). This program prepares parents and older adults to tutor learners. When she is not busy training tutors, Lee often works with small groups of learners. On several occasions, Lee is assigned responsibility for contacting new parent volunteers and orienting them to the guidelines and curriculum of the program. Her work with the PTO leads Lee to several community agencies. One of the PTO members introduces her to the coordinator of the Springfield Parent Partnership Organization, an alternative education program for single parents. Lee is able to interview several parents and recruit them for the tutoring program. She also visited and interviewed the staff at the Children's Hospital Family Crisis Center and at the Springfield Drug and Alcohol Rehabilitation Center. These experiences help Lee better understand the needs of some of her learners as well as the dynamics of the community in which they live.

Lee gathers artifacts documenting these experiences for Standard Ten in her portfolio. She wishes to demonstrate how she fosters relationships with school colleagues, parents, and agencies in the larger community and how she supported learners' achievement and well-being.

SAMPLE RATIONALE PAGE

Artifact for Standard Ten: Leadership and Collaboration
Name of Artifact: Collection of Documents from Work with PTO Afterschool Tutoring Program
Date: December 12, 2012
Course: EDE 461—Student Teaching
Rationale:

While student teaching at Springfield High School, I became involved in the afterschool tutoring program sponsored by the PTO. To document my work, I have included my volunteer's log and journal, which chronicles the experiences I had with the learners as well as with the parent volunteers. Also included are samples of learner work and a packet of materials I created to use in training parent volunteers for tutoring services.

My visits to the Springfield Parent Partnership Organization, the Children's Hospital Family Crisis Center, and the Springfield Drug and Alcohol Rehabilitation Center are documented with letters of inquiry and thank-you notes. The purpose of these visits was to enhance our tutoring program by reaching out to potential volunteers as well as to learners in need.

Finally, I have included a certificate of appreciation from the Springfield PTO. Each document portrays my ability to coordinate the efforts of parents and community members in the interest of helping learners who need tutoring in high school. I believe that programs of this type are most successful when there is a thorough understanding of the impact the community has on its children and when there is a partnership between the school and its neighboring agencies. My work with the PTO and its afterschool tutoring program reflects my commitment to this belief. The relationships that I cultivated as a result of this experience will benefit me in the future. I have learned that partnerships are essential for success in the classroom. I feel confident that I will be able to work with volunteer parent tutors in my future classroom.

TRY THIS

Balancing a Portfolio Around Teaching Standards

This is a helpful technique for initially organizing a collection of artifacts that you are considering entering into your professional portfolio and then making meaningful additions to that collection. The goal of this process is achieving a balanced portfolio where all standards are well documented and a wide variety of artifacts are used. This activity can easily be adapted to the development of electronic portfolios.

1. Label a set of expandable file folders, one folder for each of the standards you are using. For example, if you are using the InTASC standards, you would have ten labeled folders.
2. Attach a sticky note to each artifact in your current collection. On the note, list all the competencies, skills, and understandings you gained through the experience represented

by this artifact. Circle the most important of these benefits. Find the standard that is most representative of this most important competency. Drop this artifact in the file folder for that standard.

3. Make a plan for achieving a more balanced portfolio. You might decide to omit some documents that you initially intended to use because they are redundant. Then set goals for yourself that will enable you to better document underrepresented standards, using a wide variety of artifacts. These goals will enable you to chart the course of your own professional development. Let your goals guide you as you choose meetings and workshops to attend, select journals to read, consider organizations to join, exercise assignment choices wisely, and volunteer for school and community events.

4. Discuss your current artifacts and your plans for your own professional development with a mentor or instructor. You will no doubt find the insights and suggestions of another professional educator to be invaluable.

5

Artifact Possibilities

HOW TO USE THIS CHAPTER

The types of documents listed on the next few pages are possible artifacts for your portfolio. They are explained here so that you may use them to greater advantage. Each definition contains two features: a description of the document as it relates to classes and other learning opportunities and an explanation of the types of teaching skills that this document may reflect. These suggestions do not include all the possibilities that exist as documents. As you create artifacts that refer to learners or teachers, avoid using names or other identifying information. It is always critical to maintain confidentiality.

TYPES OF ARTIFACTS

Action Research

Include examples of action research, in which you have inquired about ways to improve classroom instruction, student learning, and your own practices. Your investigation can reflect work that you have done alone or as a member of a team of teachers and perhaps other professionals. You should describe how you sought to generate and sustain improvement in teaching and learning as a result of your investigation. You may also highlight certain aspects of the research. Carefully consider the nature of your inquiry and the standard that you have chosen. For example, you may want to consider describing how you progressed through the process by reflecting upon and assessing your teaching practices as you explored new ideas, implemented strategies, and utilized new resources. Regardless of which standard and aspect of inquiry you choose to highlight, remember always to address the impact of your work on learners.

Adaptations

Good teachers understand that learners with disabilities or exceptional gifts may need accommodations, adaptations, or modifications to achieve maximum development. You may have made adaptations to an activity, an assessment, a game, a teaching material, or the physical environment to accommodate the needs of one or more learners. In designing these adaptations, it is important to consider the learner's strengths as well as struggles in order to make the adaptation appropriately challenging. Documents that reflect your adaptations may demonstrate your knowledge of human development, your instructional planning skills, and certainly your ability to adapt instruction for individual needs.

Anecdotal Records

Anecdotal records are notes that you have taken in classroom observations or during your own teaching. They may pertain to any of the following: the intellectual, social, emotional, or physical development of one or more learners; personal observations about instructional decisions that you have made; or personal observations of teachers at work. The notes reflect your assessment or child observation skills, your ability to make instructional plans, and your knowledge of child development.

Article Summaries or Critiques

You may have written a summary or an evaluation of an article from a professional journal as a class assignment. When including these writings in your portfolio, choose critiques that address the desired topic very specifically. The title of the article should be reflective of a chosen standard, making an obvious connection. This document is especially helpful if your professor has made positive remarks about your work and these remarks are about the standard you wish to document.

The article summary or critique may show your ability to analyze any number of teaching skills. For example, suppose you critiqued an article titled "Getting Parents Involved in Their Children's Education." If you discussed your own ideas about parent involvement in your critique, this document may be able to reflect your knowledge of school–home–community cooperation.

Assessments

Any forms of assessment you have used or developed to measure learner performance would be included in this type of document. Examples of assessments are performance tasks, student portfolios, teacher-written tests, informal observations or notes, evaluations from lesson plans, formative assessment notes or charts, and summative charts of student developmental levels. You may want to include the actual assessment instrument you have written, with the learner's work on it, if applicable (only a few copies are necessary). In addition, you may include notes in a personal journal from observations made during the administration of a standardized test. Your ability to assess students' performance, diagnose progress, and use the data from assessments wisely is reflected in this document. In addition, your understanding of learner development may be evident.

Awards and Certificates

Copies of letters, awards, or certificates that verify your outstanding contribution to the field of education fit in this category. These could include honors conferred, memberships in honorary professional organizations, community recognition, and volunteer recognition. Your professional commitment is reflected in these types of documents.

Behavior Intervention Plans

Throughout your teaching career you will often need to develop a behavior intervention plan for managing a learner's behavior. Your plan may include strategies such as changing the environment, providing positive reinforcement, or offering support to promote acceptable classroom behavior. Your plans are shared with the learners and parents, and consequences for failure to adhere to the plan are outlined. The behavior intervention plan provides documentation of skills in motivating and managing students.

Bulletin Board Ideas

After creating a bulletin board, make a copy of your design or take a photograph of the board. Make sure all spelling, punctuation, and grammar are standard English. This document can be used to show your ability to think creatively, use materials in interesting ways, or motivate learners.

Case Studies

A case study is a thorough examination of a learner's growth over a period of time. When using this as a document, make sure the learner is anonymous. Generally, case studies are quite long; therefore, you may want to include a specific part of the paper for documentation of a standard. Your knowledge of human development as well as your observation skills may be evident in this document.

Classroom Management Philosophy

This is a written summary of your philosophy of classroom management. Make sure to cite the research and theories that have guided you in the way you influence learner behavior and encourage development of self-control. Classroom management skills and knowledge of human development are evident in this document.

Community Resources Documents

These might include copies of actual correspondence or a description of less formal contact between you and a community resource. Have you solicited a community resource to provide information in completing a course assignment or to teach a lesson in the classroom? Did you invite a guest speaker into your classroom during a field class or student teaching? These types of correspondence show that you are able to foster positive relationships between the community and the school.

Content Organizers

These instructional tools are visual and graphic representations of the content of written materials. Commonly used types of content organizers are graphic organizers, semantic maps, and story maps. The teacher creates an organizer that visually depicts the main ideas or elements of the text that the learners are to read, which requires that the teacher become familiar with the written material, its structure, and the relevant information to be gleaned from it. You may find opportunity to create a content organizer while making lesson plans for a reading lesson or for a subject area such as social studies. This could document your knowledge of a subject area and your skill in using an effective instructional strategy.

Cooperative Learning Strategies

Have you planned or taught a lesson using a cooperative learning technique? Cooperative learning is a method of teaching in which learners work collaboratively in small heterogeneous groups to solve a problem. This type of group work must be obvious in your lesson. You may want to include a copy of the lesson plan and, if the lesson was actually taught, a statement assessing the effectiveness of the cooperative learning technique. This will document your ability to use cooperative learning as a strategy as well as your ability to manage and motivate a group of learners.

Curriculum Plans

These documents are written plans, programs, or both and are designed to organize curriculum. Your curriculum plans can reflect all experiences you have developed for the learner while engaged in the process of schooling. Examples may include pacing guides, lesson plans, units, thematic units, learning centers, extracurricular programs, or school–community ventures. These documents portray your instructional planning skills or your ability to use many and varied instructional strategies.

Curriculum Plans with Culturally Responsive Focus

This type of instruction is designed to maximize the match between the home culture and the school culture. It is based on the understanding that there are many sociocultural influences on learning. When you have been successful at learning about your students' experiences and designing curriculum in which learners can see themselves reflected and respected, you have been culturally responsive. When you invite the expression of multiple perspectives on issues and model acceptance and mutual respect, you have been culturally responsive. Curricula containing culturally responsive instruction demonstrate your disposition to build partnerships with the homes and communities of your students as well as your ability to plan meaningful instruction.

Data Analyses of Student Learning

This type of document is a collection and analysis of objective, empirical data about student learning. Such data can be collected on individuals, small groups, or whole groups to differentiate instruction and guide action research. Data analysis documents your knowledge of human development and learning, your ability to adapt instruction to individual needs, and your ability to assess student learning.

Differentiated Instruction Plans

Differentiated instruction plans adjust the curriculum to the varied needs of learners based on empirical data. In these plans, teachers often present information in a variety of modalities, such as visual, auditory, and kinesthetic learning. They also use technological media to help vary their instructional presentation methods to meet the needs of all learners. Such plans can include accommodations for a variety of learning situations, including whole and small group as well as individualized instruction. Your ability to design differentiated instruction plans supports your ability to plan for instruction and address learning differences.

Essays

You can use papers from education courses, English composition, or any other class in which you were required to write an essay. Examine the topic you addressed in your paper to be sure its main idea reflects one of the standards you are using.

This type of artifact can document almost any standard. A question you wish to answer or the topic you wish to address should be clearly stated at the beginning of the essay. You may want to highlight this, showing its obvious connection to the standard you wish to document. For example, suppose you wrote an essay in a composition class titled "Why Leah Can't Do Math: The Influence of Societal Expectations." Because this is an essay on the differences that gender may make in the perception of students in the home, neighborhood, and school, your understanding of social influences on the education of females becomes evident, especially if you offer suggestions that show how you would eliminate gender bias in your own math lessons. This would be a good artifact to document your understanding of the individual needs of learners and your ability to create instructional opportunities for everyone in your class.

Evaluations

Any positive on-the-job performance assessment is an especially important type of evaluation to include in a portfolio. Student teaching is one place where this will occur. You might include actual observations done when you taught a lesson, feedback on a written assignment, or some kind of summative assessment (interim or final evaluation). Make sure there is a relationship between the evaluation comments and the standard. Typically principals evaluate teachers every year and share their observations with the teachers.

Field Trip Plans

You may have gone on field trips that would be related to one of the standards you have chosen. These kinds of trips may include visits to teacher centers, libraries, museums, innovative classrooms, other universities, youth centers, or rehabilitation centers. You may document this by including copies of programs, personal journals, agenda, letters of invitation, or memos. Your own notes or observational reports are also helpful. This type of document may provide evidence for a variety of standards. Your professional commitment and responsibility are reflected because of your willingness to seek information outside the college classroom.

If you actually planned a field trip for one of your classes, be sure to document this. Record your lesson plans, your correspondence with the community agents involved, your letters to parents, and any other communication you used. This is strong evidence of your planning skills, knowledge of content, knowledge of human development, and school–home–community cooperation.

Floor Plans

A floor plan is a sketch of the arrangement of space, equipment, and materials you designed in order to meet the needs of a group of learners under your supervision. Your ability to use environments and materials appropriately is most closely related to this document. If you include a statement of how this floor plan enhances your classroom management plan, then it also could document your classroom management skills.

Goal Statements

Professional goals are based on your needs, interests, philosophy of education, and perception of your role as a teacher. Goal statements assist you in determining where you want to be and provide you with information about how to get there.

Think about the important results you should accomplish in your role as a teacher and record these as goal statements. Remember that any short-term goals you establish should be tied to the long-term standards you have chosen to guide your professional development. Periodically review and evaluate your accomplishments in relation to your goal statements. You may wish to list your accomplishments associated with each goal. You will establish new goals as you refine your philosophy of education, your role as a teacher, and your expectations. It is important to keep your list of goal statements current. These statements might appear at the beginning of your portfolio or as documentation of your professional commitment.

Grouping Structures

Effective teachers use a variety of grouping structures to meet educational outcomes. You may wish to document your flexibility in grouping learners and your ability to create and manage different types of groups. Your documents might be lesson plans using structures such as these: whole-class instruction, same-ability groups, mixed-ability groups, cooperative learning groups, one-on-one teaching, and peer tutoring. Perhaps you have tried a variety of cooperative learning strategies such as Jigsaw or Teams-Games-Tournaments. Your lesson plans would demonstrate your classroom management and instructional planning skills as well as your ability to adapt instruction to learner differences.

Homework Assignments

You can achieve some important educational goals with carefully designed homework assignments. Some of these goals include improvements to achievement, mastery of skills, attitudes toward school, study skills, parent involvement, and self-discipline. You could document your success in this area by providing sample homework assignments or adaptations or by describing your homework practices and policies or your successes in involving parents. These documents can be used to indicate your knowledge of learner development, ability to adapt instruction for individual differences, communication or planning skills, or ability to form partnerships with the home.

Individualized Education Program

IEPs are management tools that describe the special education services appropriate to the needs of learners with disabilities. These documents delineate the present performance levels of the learner as well as measurable goals for improvement. An important aspect of these plans is how the learner's progress toward achievement of the stated goals will be measured. They outline the accommodations as well as the supports the learner will receive. IEPs are intended as a communication tool for all the educators working with a learner. If you served on a team designing an IEP for a learner or if you were an educator using an IEP to guide your practice, you can write a description of this experience for your portfolio. Remember that it is absolutely essential to maintain confidentiality when writing such a description. This type of document demonstrates your knowledge of learning development and your ability to adapt instruction for individual differences and work in partnership with other professionals and with parents.

Interviews with Learners, Teachers, Parents, or Caregivers

These interviews include planned conversations with a specific agenda. Include a copy of the questions and answers as well as a summary and analysis of the interview. This interview may be part of a case study for one of your classes. Interviews can yield a variety of information; for example, an interview with a learner may give you some indication of his or her language development, thus documenting your understanding of learner development.

Inquiry Learning Episodes

Inquiry learning is a student-centered, active-learning instructional strategy focusing on questioning, critical thinking, and problem solving. Often the topic of inquiry is specified by the teacher, but the learners form and test the hypotheses, using methods they select. Inquiry learning is most associated with the field of science, which naturally lends itself to investigation and data collecting. But inquiries often lead to connections that cross discipline lines. Unlike problem- and project-based learning, inquiry learning episodes are short term. When you document an inquiry learning episode you are providing evidence of your knowledge of instructional strategies and planning skills, ability to apply content, and management of a student-centered learning environment.

Journals

You may have kept journals during field classes or field observation assignments. Some inservice teachers find journals to be a way to track an aspect of their teaching over time. Include them if they address your observations of learners as they relate to the desired standard. If necessary, highlight the appropriate sections of the journals. Make sure dates and times are included but not the names of schools or teachers visited.

Lesson Plans

Copies of your lesson plans should include all components of a workable plan: objectives, materials, introduction, procedures, closing, and evaluation. Sometimes plans may be used for more than one standard. In this case, highlight the specific part of the plan that documents the standard. Your ability to execute instructional planning and use a variety of instructional strategies will be most obviously documented with lesson plans; however, it is possible that knowledge of content, use of environments and materials, communication skills, and knowledge of learner development can also be documented here.

Letters to Parents or Caregivers

Include copies of correspondence sent to the home. This correspondence can include permission slips, weekly newsletters, requests for help with homework, notices about parties or field trips, requests for family conferences, student award certificates, or letters that explain upcoming activities. Such correspondence can document your cooperation with the home and community as well as your communication skills. Make sure letters contain correct spelling and standard English grammar.

Management and Organization Strategies

After trying a particular management or classroom organization strategy, systematically observe and code the events that occurred. This will enable you to record what is important about your experience. Write a brief summary and explanation of your observation. For example, you may have tried a chart system for classroom jobs, a record-keeping device for holistic scoring of writing, a system of recording anecdotal notes, or a way to expedite peer editing during writing classes. These types of explanations reflect your ability to manage the classroom well.

Meetings and Workshops Log

If you have attended meetings or listened to speakers who discussed a topic related to a particular standard, include a reaction paper plus a copy of the program. These logs also would be a good way to document your professional commitment and responsibility.

Multidisciplinary Learning Plans

Multidisciplinary learning, or parallel design, is when lessons or units are developed across many disciplines with a common organizing topic by teachers of different disciplines. If you have participated in a multidisciplinary team, you could use lesson plans or a unit plan to demonstrate your ability to apply content or knowledge of multiple instructional strategies.

Observation Reports

Systematic, regular observation and recording of behaviors, events, and interactions in the classroom should be part of every teaching experience you have. Include brief descriptions of your observations in a variety of circumstances. Reports could be in paragraph or checklist format. Depending on the focus of your observations, your reports may reflect your knowledge of a variety of standards.

Parent/Caregiver–Teacher Conference Summaries

Successful conferences help parents or caregivers and teachers gain insight into student learning. Both caregivers and teachers have an opportunity to ask questions concerning behavior and share ideas about learner needs. Teachers know that successful communication involves preparation for before, during, after, and follow-up of the conference. If you are a preservice teacher, perhaps you have been invited to attend these conferences or have observed a teacher preparing for, attending, or following up on a parent/caregiver–teacher conference. Take notes and make sure they reflect the teacher's preparation for all parts of the conference. You will need to include notes on details such as the seating arrangements, the manner in which the teacher shared student progress, resolution of concerns, participants' questions, and time management. If you are including your conference notes, be sure that no forms of identification for the learner, parent or caregiver, teacher, school, or district are included. These conference summaries document your ability to establish partnerships.

Peer Critiques

Peer critiques encompass formal and informal assessments of you by your peer educators. These can include score reports that are made out by peers during your class presentations. The standard you document with this artifact depends on the presentation that your peers critique. If it was, for example, a lesson demonstration, your planning or instructional strategies skills would be evident. Your use of materials, communication skills, or knowledge of learning development might also be evident. Make sure the comments made by your peers reflect the standard you are documenting.

Philosophy Statement

This is a brief position paper or statement of your philosophy of teaching. Make it clear and concrete. You may want to preface your entire portfolio with this statement. Sometimes it is an assignment in a class, but if not, write one on your own. It should include your underlying beliefs about the teaching strategies and practices that are best for learners. Either omit or explain educational jargon; do not include such terms simply because they sound good. If you include the philosophy statement in more than one section, highlight the part that pertains to the specific standard.

Pictures and Photographs

Include photographs that show active learning in progress, special projects, field trips, or artistic expressions that cannot be physically included in your portfolio because of size. Bulletin boards, puppets, learning centers, and trips to museums are just some of the many ideas and activities that you may want to photograph. Depending on the photographs, you may be able to document a variety of standards. If the photograph is of a field trip that you took to a professional meeting or conference, document your professional commitment. If it is of a field trip or other related activity in which you participated with a class of learners, you may want to document your use of instructional strategies, depending on your involvement in the planning process.

Student Portfolios

A student portfolio is an organized collection of work that demonstrates the learner's achievement and performance over time. Various kinds of evidence might be used, including the learner's projects, written work, learning journals, and video demonstrations. A sample student portfolio documents your understanding of varied assessment strategies.

Position Papers

Include scholarly papers written to present an educational issue, viewpoint, or controversy. Be sure that sources are up to date. Position papers can document your professional commitment as well as your knowledge of philosophical and social influences.

Problem-Based Learning Curricula

Problem-based learning is a student-centered instructional strategy that is used to engage learners in investigating authentic and realistic problems. This strategy promotes active learning, the development of problem-solving skills and strategies, and higher-level thinking skills while learners master complex, multifaceted content. Key components of this strategy include defining the problem, data collection, brainstorming and researching ideas, developing and evaluating solutions, and communicating results. Your knowledge of a variety of instructional strategies, instructional planning skills, and ability to apply content and manage a student-centered learning environment should be evident from a problem-based learning artifact.

Problem-Solving Logs

As you identify professional problems or challenges, record them. It would be helpful to include a clear statement of the problem, alternative strategies for dealing with the problem, the chosen strategies, and the results of the implementation of each strategy. Depending on the problem you solved, you can document your use of instructional strategies, management of the learning environment, or cooperation with the home and community.

Professional Development Plans

Include a short paragraph or list explaining your short- and long-term plans for professional development. This list can include efforts to improve knowledge or performance in specific areas of teaching, attendance and participation in professional organizations or workshops, and plans for earning additional credits in graduate school. This area should reflect where you are now in terms of your profession and where you plan to be within the next few years. Such statements document your professional commitment and responsibility.

Professional Organizations and Committees List

List and briefly describe your involvement with an organization, committee, or other group that you feel has had an impact on you professionally or personally. Examples can include participation in campus and/or community organizations. Be sure to include evidence of your participation in these groups, such as a membership card, a letter of acceptance, or program from an activity. Such memberships show that you actively seek out opportunities to grow professionally.

Professional Readings List

Keep a list of professional readings you have done and include your reactions to the issues and concepts discussed. Your professional commitment and responsibility are reflected in professional reading lists.

Project-Based Learning Curricula

Project-based learning is a student-centered instructional strategy that engages learners in in-depth and worthwhile projects. The project is organized around one or more guiding questions that require learners to think critically and creatively while learning essential knowledge. Learners are required to create a publically presented product or performance to illustrate what they have learned. Projects are long term, interdisciplinary, and as authentic as possible. When you document a project-based learning experience, you demonstrate your knowledge of instructional strategies, skills with instructional planning and managing a student-centered learning environment, and ability to apply content.

Projects

Projects can include any type of assignment for preservice teachers or activity for inservice teachers that involved problem solving, presenting as a group, creating materials, investigating phenomena in classrooms, or researching current information. If this is a group project, make that clear but indicate the extent of your input. (Be careful about this one; it is not helpful to brag about doing all the work.) The documentation possibilities of this artifact depend on the project. Examine the standards to determine whether the project reflects instructional planning skills, professional commitment, the ability to meet individual differences, or knowledge of content.

References

References can include statements, evaluations, or both, from your supervisors of your academic work, experiences in the classroom, other work experience with children, or outside employment. Try to connect the reference with one of your selected standards. For instance, the reference might describe a lesson you taught. You can use this document to illustrate your competence in the area of instructional strategies. In addition, you may want to place reference letters from your supervisors in a special tabbed section of the portfolio.

Research Papers

When selecting a research paper to include in your portfolio, you need to consider several factors. The content of the research paper might make it appropriate for inclusion under a particular standard. It might, for instance, highlight your knowledge of an academic subject.

Rubrics

Include examples of rubrics you have developed or selected to measure student performance. You may also describe how you instructed learners to use the rubric as a tool for self-assessment. Be certain your rubric offers a set of categories that define and describe the important components of the work being assessed. This includes gradation of levels of completion or proficiency with a score assigned to each level and a description of what criteria need to be met to attain that score at each level. Because the criteria for assessment are clearly defined, you may choose to share examples of how this enabled you and your students to share a common understanding of the assignment's goals and criteria and the various levels of completing the defined criteria.

Rules and Procedures Descriptions

This type of document should describe the regular, repeated guidelines or routines for behavior that give your classroom predictability and order. These descriptions of rules should give some evidence of your ability to manage the classroom and create an environment conducive to learning and positive interaction.

Schedules

Most inservice teachers and some student teachers are asked to complete a daily schedule. If you use this as a document, be sure that it clearly describes your format for the events of the day for learners under your supervision. The order of events and the length of time allotted to each should be clear and concise. Classroom management skills are reflected in this type of artifact.

Scope-and-Sequence Charts

The scope-and-sequence chart is a graphic representation of the major elements of the curriculum. It reflects the range and depth (scope) and the order (sequence) of the curriculum. It is generally represented as a chart that displays the standards or intended outcomes learners must achieve at various grade levels. The chart can be used as a framework for curriculum planning and development that assists the teacher with monitoring curriculum changes and as he or she orients learners, parents, and other educational stakeholders to the school curriculum. This artifact can support documentation of your instructional planning skills and ability to form partnerships.

Seating-Arrangement Diagrams

A particular seating arrangement (such as having learners sit in groups) might complement a particular teaching strategy (such as cooperative learning). It might also reflect a particular classroom management need, such as seating certain learners apart from the rest of the class. Your ability to plan for instruction, use environments, and manage the classroom can be documented with this artifact.

Self-Assessment Instruments

This includes results from instruments, rating scales, surveys, or questionnaires that provide feedback about your performance. This instrument shows your professional commitment and responsibility. Self-assessment instruments also include examples of instruments you developed to engage learners in measuring their own performance (cognitive, affective, and psychomotor). These instruments can document your assessment skills.

Simulated Experiences

Include an explanation of educational experiences in which you learned through the use of simulation as a teaching method. A simulation is an activity that represents a real-life experience. This activity can include teaching an elementary lesson in a methods class, dramatizing a simulated classroom management scenario, or some other type of role-play experience. Describe the simulation, its purpose, and what you feel you learned from the experience. The simulation itself will determine the standard you can document.

Student Contracts

You may have the opportunity to write individual (one-on-one) contracts to help promote a learner's academic achievement or improved behavior. The actual contract should look formal—it should be typed, and it should specifically spell out the conditions under which the terms of the contract (achievement, behavior, and so on) will be met. In addition, it should include spaces for the teacher and the learner to sign, date, and confirm their agreement to the conditions. If you are a preservice teacher, you may not have the need to draw up contracts until you student teach, but you may see some in use during your field experiences. (Classroom management rules that all learners are expected to follow do not qualify under this category.) This type of artifact reflects your ability to develop learning experiences on the basis of diagnosis and observation, or perhaps it can document your classroom management skills, depending on the reason for the individual contract.

Student Work

The actual work that your learners produce is one of the most important indicators of your effectiveness as a teacher. You should include in your portfolio representative samples of learner projects and assignments as well as video recordings of learner performances. Whenever possible, you should include the criteria or rubric you used to evaluate this work. Your portfolio would not be complete unless it documents how you are attaining learning results while simultaneously mastering teaching competencies. Remember always to remove learners' names from their work and obtain parent or guardian permission to photograph or record.

Teacher-Made Materials

These materials may include games, manipulatives, puppets, big books, charts, videotapes, films, photographs, transparencies, teaching aids, costumes, posters, and artwork. Because many of these items are cumbersome, include only paper copies or photographs of the materials. If you do not have copies of the actual materials you have made, you may want to highlight sections of a well-designed lesson plan that show how you would use creative teaching materials. Materials that support learning theory and that were designed for this purpose are most helpful. Your materials should reflect your ability to encourage active learning and include a variety of instructional strategies.

Technological Resources

This artifact includes descriptions of a wide range of technological resources you incorporate into your instruction. Be sure to demonstrate evidence that you use these materials in a challenging and appropriate way to encourage active learning. You may also wish to include a list of the media and technology used in your classroom on a regular basis.

Theme Studies

Thematic learning is an instructional strategy that connects ways of learning and meaningful content from more than one discipline, organized around one central theme. Teachers organize the theme study to provide relevant, in-depth knowledge and transferable learning strategies and skills. Learners are required to put cognitive skills such as reading, writing, and thinking into the context of a real-life situation. Learning is kept holistic, crossing discipline lines where it is natural to do so. Your knowledge of a variety of instructional strategies, instructional planning skills, and ability to manage student-centered learning environments and apply content should be evident from your theme studies.

Unit Plans

A unit is an integrated plan for instruction on a topic developed over several days or even weeks. Often, units are interdisciplinary, and lessons are organized to build on knowledge acquired in previous lessons. Unit plans generally include purposes, objectives, content outlines, activities, instructional resources, and evaluation methods. Unit plans document your ability to use a variety of instructional strategies and instructional planning skills.

Video Scenario Critiques

Often in university methods courses, professors will ask you to view and critique a video of actual teaching scenarios. If you wish to include a critique you have completed, be sure to describe the scenario and give its bibliographical information. Make sure the critique addresses the standard you plan to document. Depending on the nature of the video, there are several possibilities for documentation.

Volunteer Experience Descriptions

These documents might include a list and brief description of volunteer experiences and services provided to the school and community. You should focus on how these activities have enhanced your teaching abilities while providing a contribution to society. You should also emphasize the importance of maintaining positive school–community collaboration through teacher, parent/caregiver, and learner interaction.

Work Experience Descriptions

These written statements describe your work experiences. These might include work with learners in both traditional and nontraditional settings and work for which you were compensated or that you performed on a voluntary basis. To be of most interest, these statements should include not only a summary of the setting and your responsibilities but also a reflective statement addressing the intangible aspects of the work experience. In writing these statements, be sure to address how these work experiences relate to the specific standard.

6

Using the Portfolio Throughout a Teaching Career

THE FULL POTENTIAL OF PORTFOLIOS

A portfolio is a "proving tool." It provides a body of evidence regarding your professional competencies; in addition, it enables you to be self-aware and self-reflective as you teach. A well-developed portfolio can offer one unique picture of what successful teaching looks like.

However, an effective portfolio is not about putting on a good face to appear more competent than you actually are in order to sell yourself to others. To be powerful, a portfolio must be a truthful self-portrait that gives others an accurate picture of where you are in the lifelong journey of professional development. Because it is truthful, it gains the ability to be an "improving tool" as well as a "proving tool." At its best, a portfolio charts an important developmental process in which goals are continually reached and new goals for improvement are set. Portfolio work should raise as many questions as it answers about effective teaching.

Throughout your entire teaching career, you will want to know how well you are doing and be able to show others where you are as a professional. For this reason, portfolio work should last the duration of your career. However, your professional portfolio will evolve as your career advances. Its purposes change; the artifacts chosen for inclusion will change; perhaps your organizational system will change in time. The purpose of this chapter is to show how you can best use a portfolio throughout your career—while studying in a teacher preparation program, while searching for a teaching job, and while serving in a teaching position.

USING THE PORTFOLIO WHILE IN A TEACHER EDUCATION PROGRAM

Creating a professional portfolio requires a great deal of time and hard work. In this chapter, you will be introduced to several motivating reasons for you to commit time, energy, and thought to developing a portfolio. In a portfolio, you will have a high-impact, authentic product by which your professional competence can be understood by yourself and judged by others.

Using a Portfolio to Understand the Profession

As you build a record of your professional growth in a portfolio, you will also come to understand the big picture of the teaching profession. You are well advised to build your portfolio around widely accepted standards for the profession. Standards will help you have the end in mind as you study to be a teacher. By focusing on standards, you will gain a vision of the destination toward which you are traveling. As you document these standards, you will better understand the roles and responsibilities of a teacher. Your documents will show what competent practice of these standards might look like in actual behavior. Furthermore, as you organize selected artifacts around these standards, you will begin to discern a pattern of how various course assignments and out-of-class experiences fit into this big picture and contribute to your professional development.

Using a Portfolio to Gain Self-Understanding

You will find as you engage in portfolio development that you gain a clear picture of yourself as an emerging professional. Your portfolio will provide a record of quantitative and qualitative growth over time in your selected goal areas or standards. A portfolio allows you to see a profile of your strengths and weaknesses. As you connect your work to standards, you can see the value and relevance of your work. A portfolio enables you to reflect on the significance of everyday assignments and experiences with learners. You will recognize the value of many out-of-class experiences, such as volunteer work, and you can generate documents to reflect the value of these experiences. In time, you gain an understanding of where you are and where you are headed. Your portfolio will give you insights into your philosophy and value system as you reflect on what you have found worth documenting. When you take seriously the value of written reflections on your documents, your portfolio can serve as a scaffold for clarifying your personal teaching philosophy. A portfolio provides a trail of evidence of your progress that will give you a sense of accomplishment and pride. As you gain self-awareness and self-confidence in your professional abilities, you can assume more responsibility for your own continuous professional development. A portfolio helps you focus on what is important to you. Then you can clearly define what you want to accomplish and can take the initiative to achieve this.

Using a Portfolio to Design Your Own Professional Growth

As you gain more self-understanding, you will become empowered to assume more control over your future learning. You can become a proactive negotiator of your professional development because you have a clear vision of your destination and your goals. To the extent that you have gained an understanding of the profession and of yourself within the profession, you will be equipped to collaborate with professors in individualizing assignments or with advisors in planning a course of study. You and your cooperating teachers in student teaching or early field experiences have a tool in the portfolio for determining the most appropriate teaching experiences for you. When you reflect on the portrait that your portfolio provides, you will be well positioned to set realistic and meaningful goals for yourself. Autonomous adult learners with an understanding of their profession and of themselves are proactive in all choices and decisions to be made in their education. They enter every learning experience with clear goals in mind. Other ways to become proactive include inviting a professional to be your mentor, developing a peer support group for portfolio work, searching for field placements to best meet your needs, suggesting possible research topics to professors, initiating your own volunteer experiences, and developing a personal professional reading agenda.

Using the Portfolio to Gain Holistic, Authentic Assessment

Unlike many other forms of assessment, portfolios can capture the complexities of teaching. They have the unique power to make your learning visible. Some teacher preparation programs have portfolio assessment systems in place. In such programs, portfolios will provide faculty members with evidence of their effectiveness in preparing learners to meet selected standards. Even if your teacher education program doesn't require portfolios, you should be proactive in presenting your portfolio to others who are assessing your development. For example, you might share your portfolio at an interview where others are determining your readiness for student teaching. It is also advisable to share your portfolio with supervising teachers at field sites and student teaching sites. When you present a portfolio, you are enabling others to assess you broadly, completely, and fairly.

When portfolio work is ongoing throughout your entire teacher education program, your portfolio becomes a powerful tool for enabling you to understand yourself and your profession, become a proactive architect of your own professional development, and obtain fair and comprehensive assessment of your competence. At the end of your teacher education program, you will have a presentation portfolio that can easily be adapted as an interview tool. However, having an interview portfolio does not guarantee having a successful interview. Interviewing with a portfolio requires thoughtful planning.

USING THE PORTFOLIO WHEN INTERVIEWING FOR A TEACHING POSITION

Imagine for a moment that you have arrived at an interview for your first teaching position. You are on time, professionally dressed, and armed with a well-developed portfolio. Your interviewer invites you to sit down and begins to ask a barrage of questions. Your mind goes blank; you do not know how to respond to most of the questions. After stammering through them as best you can, you realize that no one has asked to look at your portfolio. Before leaving, you ask the interviewer if he would like to see it. "I'm sure it's really interesting. However, I have several other interviews today and can't spend the time browsing through your portfolio right now. Thanks anyway," he says. You leave with confidence shaken, feeling quite sure that you will not be hired for the position. How can you avoid such a scenario?

It is imperative to prepare. Your professional appearance and your neatly organized portfolio will probably not be enough. You will need to plan ways to effectively handle questions and incorporate the portfolio into your interview responses. This enables you to present yourself as an effective communicator who can offer specific, concrete documentation of your teaching abilities. Most interviewers prefer that you reference the portfolio during the interview, rather than simply offering it to them to peruse. This saves them time; more important, it shows them how well you communicate. Some interviewers may ask you to leave your portfolio with them so that they can later examine it on their own. If your portfolio is on a CD or flash drive, you can give each interviewer a copy, or better yet, send them a copy prior to the interview. You can also provide a uniform resource locator (URL) if you used a web-based program to construct your portfolio. Regardless of the situation in which you find yourself, you can utilize your portfolio to your advantage during the interview—if you are properly prepared.

Before the Interview

To use your portfolio as an interviewing tool, you will need to do the following well before the interview takes place:

1. Streamline the portfolio so that it contains only the most pertinent documents, based on questions that you anticipate.
2. Create a brochure that summarizes your presentation portfolio. (See Appendix B for guidance on how to create this brochure.)
3. Plan a response to each anticipated question that incorporates your portfolio documents.

Using your portfolio as an interviewing tool means that you will need to present it in a concise and thoughtful manner. To do so, it is necessary to think about the types of questions that will likely be asked in your interview. This can help you streamline the portfolio so that it is a compact picture of your professionalism. Then you will need to be thoroughly knowledgeable about its contents so that, as you answer the interviewer's questions, you can support your responses with documents and access them instantly. All of this can help you accomplish your goal in the interview—getting the job. Let's look now at the three steps to preparing for the interview with the portfolio.

STREAMLINE THE PORTFOLIO. Portfolios can be intimidating to interviewers. Imagine walking into an interview carrying a portfolio that looks like the large-print version of the collected works of Shakespeare and includes every valued document and artifact generated during your teacher education program. You are understandably proud of it, and you may want the interviewer to see all that you have accomplished. Unfortunately, no one will ever be as impressed with your work as you, and no one will be interested in sitting down and examining every single artifact you have included in your portfolio.

The first step, therefore, in preparing for an interview is to reduce the artifacts in your portfolio to a number that will both support your responses to the interview questions and provide adequate documentation of your strengths and accomplishments as a teacher. This can be a difficult and painful process, for it means removing from the portfolio artifacts and documents in which you invested much time and energy. However, keep in mind that the purpose of the interview presentation portfolio is to showcase your professional competence, and the portfolio will not serve this purpose if its size and the number of documents in it overwhelm an interviewer.

A good guideline would be to have no more than two documents or artifacts for each standard contained in your portfolio. Were you to use the ten standards presented in this book, your presentation portfolio would contain no more than twenty artifacts. You should be able to select twenty artifacts that provide a complete picture of your professional skills and abilities. These artifacts will have to be selected with care and tailored to the specific position for which you are interviewing. Thus, an interview for a kindergarten teaching position might call for artifacts different from those appropriate for an interview for a sixth-grade teaching position. Or when interviewing with an inner-city school district, you might use different documents from those used with a rural district.

We suggest that your final selections reflect the questions you anticipate being asked in the interview so that you will be able to present solid documentation of your responses. Such hands-on evidence of your abilities will be appreciated by your interviewers and will showcase your strengths in a compelling way. There are two types of questions that you can expect: general and philosophical questions related to best practice and questions of a more personal nature that address your uniqueness.

GENERAL AND PHILOSOPHICAL QUESTIONS.   Interviewers will want to gain insight into the kind of educator you are; thus, they will ask questions that probe your knowledge of learning and your disposition toward teaching. What are they looking for?

In general, administrators hire candidates who espouse a practical orientation toward schooling. Interpersonal communication and classroom management are extremely important; therefore, it only makes sense to include at least one artifact in your portfolio that shows evidence of your communication and management skills. Besides looking for these capabilities, interviewers seek candidates who have adopted the idea that effective teaching is a blend of a variety of direct instruction and facilitative approaches conducted within a sensitive and supportive environment. Essentially, your interviewer wants to see that you are competent in all of the roles of teaching reflected in the standards that comprise your portfolio: planning, assessing, instructing, managing, and forming partnerships.

While administrators place great value on what you know about specific instructional strategies such as cooperative learning, problem solving, critical thinking, and educational technologies, they may also want to know what you have to say about philosophical orientations to teaching and learning. However, they are usually not interested in your ability to label pedagogical or philosophical camps but rather that you can demonstrate how your classroom practices are based on sound theory. Your interviewer will likely be interested in your understanding of teaching as a reflective practice in which you use a variety of instructional strategies within a cohesive philosophy that meets the needs of all learners in the classroom.

Because of this emphasis on your capabilities in the classroom, administrators will want to know about your actual experiences there. Your interviewer will most likely place great importance on any information that you offer about student teaching and field work and will rely on your cooperating teachers' evaluations of your work in their classrooms.

QUESTIONS ABOUT YOUR UNIQUENESS. Your interviewer will be interested in your teaching ability; however, he or she may be even more interested in the kind of person you are. Questions about your uniqueness will probably be an important part of your interview. You may be asked about your strengths and weaknesses, likes and dislikes, personal goals, the things that motivate you, and the way in which you work with others. For some interviewers, these are high-priority questions because they are trying to determine how well you will "fit" on a team or how well you will represent the school district to parents.

You will want to be prepared to show evidence of your unique strengths. In particular, many interviewers will look to the portfolio for evidence of the attributes about you that make you different from the other candidates. They are interested in documents that reflect, among other things, creativity, positive attitude, professionalism, organizational skills, writing ability, technology skills, potential to succeed, goal setting, leadership, effort, achievements, honors, and awards.

Therefore, before the interview takes place, study your portfolio and look for documents in your portfolio that would support your answers to these two types of questions. Commonly asked questions are listed in Figures 6.1 and 6.2. Corresponding supporting portfolio documents are listed next to each question; the source of these document types is the artifact possibilities list in Chapter 5 of this text. We have listed only the documents that would reflect authentic and practical work with children, teachers, and parents because these are the documents that administrators are most interested in seeing as part of your portfolio. Keep in mind that because your portfolio is unique, you may have other documents that will support these questions equally well. Appropriate InTASC standard numbers are listed next to each of the anticipated questions so that you can refer to those sections in your portfolio for additional documents. Figure 6.1 lists questions of a general and philosophical nature. Figure 6.2 shows anticipated questions that focus on the teacher candidate as a person. Check your portfolio against these two lists. You will see how well it can be used as an interviewing tool.

After you have examined the charts in Figure 6.1 and Figure 6.2, do some investigating. Find out some information about the school district to which you are applying. Your interviewer will want to know if you are the right person for the particular position that is available in that school district, so questions that relate to the specific programs in place at the school, questions about the local community, and even questions about textbooks that are used by the school may be asked. Many school districts have websites that offer such information. Other sources of information are the school district office, the school secretary, neighbors in the community, school board meetings, parent–teacher organization (PTO) or parent–teacher association (PTA) meetings, and even the community newspaper. Visit the school district office before your interview and ask for copies of information sent to new parents in the district, curriculum guides, or newsletters. You can also find out the names of textbooks used in the school and obtain copies of them.

You may have some strong documents that support your answers to these specific questions, depending on your student teaching experiences and university classwork. Did you do any textbook evaluations or comparisons? Did you use any curriculum guides or teachers' editions of books? Did you work with any assessment tools or tests that are used by this district? Did you complete projects that involved working with children in settings similar to the district? Look back at your work with these materials and reflect on them. Include documents that will support answers to questions that you anticipate from

Anticipated Questions of a General/ Philosophical Nature	InTASC Standard(s)	Supporting Portfolio Documents
What is your educational philosophy?	(Varies according to your philosophical orientation and how you present it.)	Article summaries or critiques Anecdotal records Essays Letters to parents Philosophy statement
What does an ideal classroom look like?	1, 3, 5, 7, 8	Bulletin board ideas Essays Floor plans Lesson plans Letters to parents Management and organization strategies Observation reports Pictures and photographs Portfolios (learner) Projects (performance based) Seating arrangement diagrams Teacher-made materials Theme studies Unit plans
How do you assess children's work?	2, 6	Assessments (formal and informal) Case studies Diagnostic assessments Individualized education plans Interviews with learners, teachers, parents Lesson plans Portfolios (learner) Problem-solving logs Projects (performance based)
How do you work with parents and other members of the community?	10	Community resources documents Field trip plans Interviews with learners, teachers, parents Letters to parents Problem-solving logs List of professional organizations and committees Projects Volunteer experience descriptions

FIGURE 6.1 Anticipated Questions of a General/Philosophical Nature and Possible Portfolio Documents to Support Your Answers

Anticipated Questions of a General/ Philosophical Nature	InTASC Standard(s)	Supporting Portfolio Documents
How would you handle discipline problems? How would you manage your classroom? What kinds of management strategies do you like to use?	3	Classroom management philosophy Cooperative learning strategies Field trip plans Floor plans Journals Letters to parents Management and organization strategies Observation reports Pictures and photographs Problem-solving logs Grouping structures References Rules and procedures descriptions Schedules Seating arrangement diagrams Learner contracts
Explain what you know about using technology in the classroom.	5, 8	Computer programs Media competencies Projects References
What kinds of instructional strategies do you use? When? How well do they work?	8	Curriculum plans Evaluations Lesson plans Observation reports Peer critiques Pictures and photographs Projects References Teacher-made materials Theme studies Unit plans
How do you meet individual needs in the classroom?	2	Individualized education plans Interviews with learners, teachers, parents Journals Lesson plans Portfolios (learner) Problem-solving logs References Learner contracts
What textbooks and other resources have you used in the classroom? How do they compare to others?	4, 5, 7, 8	Curriculum plans Projects Theme studies Unit plans

FIGURE 6.1 (*continued*)

Anticipated Questions That Focus on Your Uniqueness	InTASC Standards	Supporting Portfolio Documents
What are your strengths? What is your greatest weakness?	(Varying, depending on your strengths.)	Awards/certificates Evaluations Goal statements Homework Letters to parents Media competencies Peer critiques Problem-solving logs Professional organizations and committees list References Self-assessment instruments Transcripts Volunteer experience descriptions Work experience descriptions
How well can you work with other people?	9, 10	Community resources documents Evaluations Field trip plans Letters to parents Peer critiques Professional organizations and committees list Projects References Volunteer experience descriptions Work experience descriptions
Tell me about yourself.	9, 10	Awards/certificates Essays Goal statements Letters to parents Peer critiques Self-assessment instruments Subscriptions Transcripts
Do you plan to go back to college for an advanced degree? What do you do to keep yourself up to date?	9	Meetings and workshops log Professional development plans Professional organizations and committees list Professional readings list Self-assessment instruments Subscriptions

FIGURE 6.2 Anticipated Questions That Focus on Your Uniqueness and Possible Portfolio Documents to Support Your Answers

Anticipated Questions That Focus on Your Uniqueness	InTASC Standards	Supporting Portfolio Documents
What work reflected in your portfolio gives you the most pride?	(Varies according to your answer.)	(A great variety of documents is possible; this depends on your value judgment.)
What did your supervisors say about your work?	9, 10	Awards/certificates Evaluations References Volunteer experience descriptions Work experience descriptions
What do people appreciate about you?	9, 10	Evaluations Peer critiques References Volunteer experience descriptions Work experience descriptions
What are your goals?	9	Goal statements Philosophy statement Professional development plans Self-assessment instruments
What is your favorite subject or topic to teach? Why?	4, 5, 9	Article summaries or critiques Awards/certificates Computer programs Essays Journals Meetings and workshops log Philosophy statement Pictures and photographs Professional readings list Research papers Self-assessment instruments Subscriptions Transcripts
What is your greatest career or academic achievement?	9, 10	Awards/certificates Evaluations Journals Peer critiques Pictures and photographs References

FIGURE 6.2 (*continued*)

that particular school district. As another example, suppose you discover that the school district to which you are applying has recently adopted a new hands-on science program. Because of the expense and time put into such a program, it is likely that administrators will be interested in knowing how well you will work with such a program. Thus, you might include a unit plan that you completed during student teaching that shows your use of hands-on strategies for teaching the processes of science. The research that you conduct on the school district to which you are applying should guide you in streamlining the contents of your portfolio.

Keep in mind that interviewers are most interested in seeing documents that show authenticity—your capabilities in working well with people and doing real teaching tasks. You may have completed some performance assessments in your education methods classes at the university; these are designed to show your capabilities in the field. Be sure to include documents that show your involvement with teaching, assessing, or observing children, as well as documents that relate to your work with parents and teachers. These documents would be most important and would take priority over documents such as research papers or essays, which tend to be vicarious rather than experiential.

Once you have found the documents that you can use during your interview to support your answers to possible questions, you need to know exactly where they are located in the portfolio. Remember, administrators are busy people; some of them may even view the portfolio as detrimental to your interview if you are fumbling for documents. Thus, you will need to be able to access documents quickly. Because your portfolio is organized around standards, you have the advantage of having your documents filed under appropriate tabs. Make sure that you know the standard numbers, their corresponding standard categories, and the documents that you have filed there. If you have created an electronic portfolio, you can arrange your home page, CD, or flash drive so that each standard is listed, with supporting documents listed directly beneath the standards, much like a table of contents. You or your interviewers can quickly access the document that the interviewers wish to see.

Another way to be sure that your portfolio serves you well in the interview is to summarize its most important contents on one page. We suggest the use of a brochure called "Portfolio at a Glance."

CREATE A BROCHURE.   The "Portfolio at a Glance" (see the end of Appendix B) allows you to present your most important artifacts in an outline format far more accessible than the complete portfolio. Interviewers might not have the time or the inclination to read the entire contents of a portfolio, but they would find it easy to examine brief descriptions of your significant documents. The brochure is also a potentially far less cumbersome tool to use in an interview situation. Instead of always trying to find a document in a large notebook or on a computer, the artifact can easily be referred to in the brochure. The brochure is something that you can provide every individual participating in the interview and hiring process.

Appendix B provides detailed directions on how to construct a "Portfolio at a Glance." The structure of the brochure is quite simple. You select two artifacts for every standard in your portfolio. Selection of the artifacts used in the brochure should correspond to those you have selected for your interview portfolio. Include in the brochure the names of the documents. Identify the teaching behaviors exemplified in the artifacts. Create a phrase that summarizes and highlights the teaching behaviors you believe each artifact demonstrates. Write two to four statements that describe in more detail the experiences, assignments, and activities undertaken in the creation of the artifact.

The front of the brochure can be personalized in a number of different ways. An email address can be added to your name, address, and phone number. A picture of you in a classroom with children could substitute for the clip art in our example. Anyone examining the brochure would then be able to connect the accomplishments described in the brochure to a name and face. There are other possibilities for the front of the brochure. You might want to quote your mission statement or key concepts from your philosophy. You might want to identify the source of the standards you are using to demonstrate your knowledge of current educational practice. If you have developed a website that includes your professional portfolio, you will want to prominently display its address on the front of your brochure. Also be sure to include a brief set of instructions on accessing your files.

Our sample brochure contains twenty artifacts, two for each of the ten InTASC standards. It does not matter how many standards your portfolio contains because the format of the brochure is flexible. The advantages of the brochure lie in its size and accessibility. Multiple copies can be produced and distributed before and during a job interview. The brochure can be attached to a résumé and mailed to prospective employers. While computer software makes producing a brochure a little easier, wonderful examples have been created without it.

PLAN PORTFOLIO-SUPPORTED RESPONSES TO ANTICIPATED QUESTIONS.   Your portfolio is an effective way to present a portrait of your professionalism. When you are asked a question and the answer is supported in your portfolio, you can take the opportunity to point out this document. We have found that most interviewers prefer that candidates use their portfolio in the interview to add strength to their answers because doing so presents the candidate as an articulate and well-prepared professional.

Suppose your interviewer asks, "How do you motivate children to learn?" You can simply answer the question, explaining your philosophy of teaching and perhaps describing one of your experiences. But using the portfolio can make your answer come alive and can provide your interviewer with concrete evidence of your capabilities.

To use our example, suppose you taught an exciting lesson during student teaching that utilized the children's interest in a subject. You could say, "One of the most important ways to get children motivated to learn is to interest them. I taught a lesson last semester in which I capitalized on the interests of my fourth graders. I spent a few minutes with them prior to the lesson, brainstorming some topics that would be applicable to my objective, and then used these topics as choices for their written reports. This plan, along with some pictures and samples of learner work, is in my portfolio."

To successfully use the technique of referencing your portfolio, you need to rehearse your interview. Your posture, your body language, and your verbal responses all need a trial run prior to your appointment. You should do this by rehearsing, first alone and then with a trusted friend or colleague.

One of the best ways to rehearse alone is to use visual imagery. Close your eyes and picture yourself smartly dressed and confident. Imagine yourself arriving at the interview site a few minutes early. Now, in your mind's eye, picture yourself from the moment you walk in the door to the moment the interview concludes. Put yourself in the best possible scenario, one in which you are in control of your answers. Picture your interviewer, who

---

Peer Feedback Form: Mock Teacher Interview

---

1. What does my nonverbal communication portray?
   Do I look confident? Nervous? Attentive?

   What suggestions can you make for improving my nonverbal communication?

2. What is my voice quality?
   Do I sound confident? Nervous? Enthusiastic?

   What suggestions can you make for improving my voice?

3. How well do I use my portfolio in the interview?
   Is my use of documents smooth and quick? Do I appear to know the contents of the portfolio well?

4. What suggestions can you make for improving my use of the portfolio in the interview?

FIGURE 6.3 Peer Feedback Form for Making Suggestions after a Mock Interview

is pleased with your answers and impressed with your portfolio. This positive visual imagery is an important step in building your confidence.

Next, rehearse with a trusted friend or colleague. Give him or her a list of questions that you anticipate. Practice answering those questions, using portfolio documents to support two or three answers. Remember to use standard English as you talk, look your interviewer in the eye, and straighten your posture. Ask for honest and constructive feedback. It may be helpful for your mock interviewer to write down some suggestions. Figure 6.3 shows a feedback form that facilitates this process.

MAKE YOUR PORTFOLIO AVAILABLE FOR PREVIEWING. Some administrators who frequently conduct interviews highly recommend that you make the portfolio available to them prior to your interview. Many interviewers make it a practice to review the candidate's résumé a day or two before an interview. If a portfolio were available at that time, it could also be reviewed at the interviewer's leisure.

One of the advantages of creating an electronic portfolio is that it makes this step of the process very simple; you can simply leave the interviewer with a labeled CD or flash drive on which you have saved your portfolio, or send a URL if your portfolio is online. Be sure to also include a short letter that introduces yourself. In this letter, be specific. Address it to the person in charge of the interview, and specify the teaching position for which you are applying. Also make sure to include brief, clear instructions for accessing your electronic portfolio.

If your portfolio consists of hard copies in a notebook, decide if you are comfortable leaving it with others. If you are, we recommend that you make available your brochure, your portfolio, and an introductory letter about three days before the interview.

If you have both types of portfolios—a notebook of hard copies and its electronic equivalent—leave the CD, flash drive, or URL with your interviewers so that they can access it prior to the interview. Also leave an introductory letter in which you give instructions for accessing the electronic file. In the letter, advise the recipient that you have a notebook of hard copies that you will bring with you to the interview.

PAY ATTENTION TO YOUR DEMEANOR. Even before the interview begins, judgments may be made about you. Your appearance, your punctuality, how you spent time while waiting for the interview, your handshake, and the way in which you filled out any application forms are all part of the total picture that you present of yourself. It is important to remember that your interviewer is not the only person making these judgments: Secretaries, receptionists, and faculty members who meet you as you enter their offices will also note your demeanor.

It is extremely important to be punctual; therefore, make sure that you arrive just a bit early. Ten to fifteen minutes of cushion time will enable you to circumvent any unforeseen situations that might occur, such as traffic jams, making a wrong turn, or spilling coffee on your suit. Be careful not to arrive too early, though, because this can interrupt the business of the office.

Once you have arrived, use this time wisely. If you must wait for your interview, seize the opportunity to learn more about the school district. Often lobby areas have newsletters, yearbooks, bulletins, or other such printed material on display and available to the public. These publications can offer valuable information about the school in which you would like to teach, and reading them while you are waiting is just one subtle way of showing your potential employer that you are truly interested in this position.

If you are asked to fill out any application forms or paperwork, pay attention to your handwriting. After all, this is a teaching position that you seek; neatness and letter formation are important, especially in the elementary grades. Someone will notice if your writing is illegible or sloppy.

Be alert. Seat yourself so that you can see and hear as much as possible. You will want to be ready when your name is called and you are invited into the interviewing room. Offer your hand for a handshake and make it firm.

INTRODUCE YOUR PORTFOLIO. Interviewers indicate that it is not uncommon for an applicant to bring a portfolio into an interview and then never refer to it. Other applicants mention the portfolio only at the end of the interview when time is short. It is a mistake to assume that an interviewer will initiate questions or comments about your portfolio. Also, be aware that time allocations are usually fixed. For these reasons, it is important at the beginning of the interview to indicate that you are prepared with a professional portfolio. There are always a few moments of introductions and informal conversation at the beginning of an interview. During this time, make a simple statement such as, "Today I have brought my professional portfolio organized around ten national standards for beginning teachers. Here is a brochure outlining the contents of my portfolio. I would be happy to share with you anything from my portfolio that interests you or to circulate my portfolio."

Then follow the interviewer's lead in these matters. A well-prepared brochure captures your portfolio in a concise and intriguing way and is likely to invite questions about the work reflected in your portfolio. Even if you never have the opportunity to circulate your portfolio, your interviewer will have in hand an effective summary of your competencies in addressing important standards for teachers. The brochure will also be a helpful reference for you to use should you want to quickly locate a particular artifact during the interview. Administrators have told us that they value this type of initiative by the candidate. Introducing your portfolio and presenting a brochure that summarizes your portfolio show that you are organized, politely assertive, capable of summarizing a lot of information, and truly interested in getting this job.

LISTEN FOR PROBES. Often the interviewer will ask a question and, upon receiving your answer, will ask you to pursue your answer further. This is a probe and an opportunity to use your portfolio to your advantage. For example, suppose the interviewer asks, "How well can you work with others?" You answer by saying, "I am a real team player. I enjoy group work because it gives me the chance to combine my talents with those of other people to get things done." Then your interviewer probes, "Well, what kinds of groups have you worked with? Tell me more about them." This is where your portfolio will be very handy. You can say, "In my portfolio, filed under 'Standard Ten, Leadership and Collaboration,' I have included a project that I completed while in college. It is a thematic unit book that three of my colleagues and I worked on together for an entire semester. It is quite a collaborative effort because the entire team was responsible for making it a success. As you can see, it contains lots of valuable resources for teaching a unit on the environment. In fact, my supervising teacher asked to borrow it for a unit she did with her fifth graders and was very excited about it. She even mentioned it in her reference letter, which is also filed under 'Standard Ten.'"

Such probes invite you to support your answers with additional information, which is the purpose of bringing your portfolio to the interview. Listen carefully for these opportunities and point out any supporting documents that you can. It is not necessary to physically locate each artifact that you mention; in fact, you will want to let the interviewer decide whether to look at these documents. What's most important is that you tell him or her that the information is there and available for careful scrutiny if needed.

EMPHASIZE YOUR PRACTICAL EXPERIENCES. All of the work that you have showcased in your portfolio is important. However, your interviewers will be most interested in work that is authentic and reflective of the tasks that teachers do on a daily basis. Thus, whenever you can, back up your answers with documentation from field work and student teaching. When appropriate, point out the reference letters that you have received from cooperating teachers, as well as any performance-based documents you have.

If you answer a question philosophically, be sure to follow up by showing the interviewer your actual experiences. For example, suppose you are asked, "What is your philosophy of teaching?" To emphasize your practical experiences, you could say, "I believe that children learn best when they are actively engaged. My teaching style reflects this. This document, filed under Standard 8, shows how I used a variety of strategies in a simulated experience that I did with third graders in my field class. We simulated events that took place on Ellis Island in the early 1900s; then the learners were required to write reports about topics related to immigration. Strategies used include brainstorming, predicting, building background knowledge, and role playing. I felt that it was important to get the learners involved in the subject before having them write, so I chose to use these simulations rather than simply assign reports and have the learners research information. There are some pictures of the simulated experiences and the bulletin board we created, as well as samples of their reports. This is just one example of how my philosophy of teaching emerges when I teach."

MAKE ALL OF YOUR RESPONSES POSITIVE ONES. Answer the questions honestly, but answer in positive tones. No one likes to be asked, "What is your greatest weakness?" However, this is a very popular interview question. You will need to be prepared to answer it positively. One way to do this is to turn your weaknesses into goals to be met. For example, if managing classroom behavior was not one of your strengths during student teaching, you could say, "One of my biggest challenges during student teaching was maintaining classroom discipline. I have begun reading some literature on this, and my goal for this year is to prevent discipline problems before they begin." You may even want to show your interviewer a document in your portfolio that lists your goals for improving your work in the classroom. In this way, you can show your interviewers that you view weaknesses as opportunities to learn and grow.

After the Interview

Going to an interview is like running a marathon; the best part is when it's over. But your sense of relief and satisfaction will be enhanced if you plan to do a few tasks. First, if you are using a paper-based portfolio, you need to make a decision about leaving it with your interviewer. Then, regardless of what you do with the portfolio, you need to be sure to leave your "Portfolio at a Glance" brochure. Finally, after you leave, you need to write a follow-up letter. Let's take a look at each of these steps.

MAKE A DECISION ABOUT LEAVING YOUR PORTFOLIO. Sometimes interviewers wish to spend more time with the portfolio and may ask you to leave it with them. If you have an electronic portfolio, your decision is easy. Simply leave a CD, flash drive, or brochure and some written instructions for accessing the portfolio. If your portfolio is not electronic, you will need to give this issue some thought prior to the interview. Again, decide what you feel comfortable doing. If you do not wish to part with your portfolio, you might suggest that you bring it back at another time or offer to leave it and pick it up later the same day. Another suggestion is to simply say, "I will need to keep my portfolio, but I can leave copies of my brochure, which summarizes its contents." You may also offer to send copies of any documents in the portfolio that intrigue the interviewer.

If you do decide that you are willing to leave your portfolio with the interviewer, be sure to make copies of all documents before you go to the interview so that you can duplicate the portfolio if necessary.

LEAVE A BROCHURE. By all means, leave your "Portfolio at a Glance" brochure when the interview is over. Because the brochure highlights your capabilities and shows how you have documented the standards that govern your teacher education program, it is a strong advocate for you in your absence. We suggest leaving a folder or a bound booklet that contains the brochure as well as any other important documents that highlight your achievements and capabilities, such as your résumé, copies of transcripts, and letters of reference. Many school districts require that you submit credentials such as the transcript prior to the interview. Thus, these documents may already be available for your interviewers. However, you may want to ask if there are any other documents that would interest the interviewers and offer to send them right away.

WRITE A FOLLOW-UP LETTER.   All of the authors of this text are parents; thus, we cannot resist the opportunity to tell you, "Be sure to say 'thank you.'" As any parent can tell you, writing a letter of thanks is simply the courteous thing to do. After all, in many school districts, competition for teaching positions is fierce, and your interviewers spend lots of time and energy preparing for and conducting interviews. Thank them for the opportunity to talk with them.

A follow-up letter will certainly enhance the impression you have made on your interviewers. It also gives you one more chance to remain in contact with them. In your letter, after saying thank you, you can summarize the highlights of your interview, making sure to mention a document or two in your portfolio. This will help the interviewer remember you, as well as showcase your communication skills.

You should be proud of this milestone you have reached. Graduation from college says many things about you—among them, your perseverance, your academic strengths, and your professional capabilities. With this achievement, you face yet another test—that of getting the job you want. Because you have a portfolio that is organized around teaching standards, you are already well prepared. Using the steps shown in this chapter, you can customize that portfolio to reflect the position you seek and utilize it as a powerful tool during the interview. This, along with some thoughtful self-reflection, will make your interview a positive and empowering experience.

USING THE PORTFOLIO DURING INSERVICE TEACHING

Once you are hired and begin your professional career as a teacher, you will continue to find the portfolio useful in many ways. The professional portfolio is changing the way teaching is being conducted and assessed. Through the use of evidenced-based documents and factual profiles, teachers are now able to offer authentic and holistic evidence of their teaching effectiveness. The professional portfolio chronicles a teacher's professional development and showcases his or her pedagogy. It is a catalyst for refining one's teaching philosophy and goals and for improving teaching practices.

The professional portfolio will assist you throughout your teaching career. First-year teachers, their assigned mentors, and administrators use portfolios to assist in the induction process. Beginning and veteran teachers have found portfolios useful in defining and managing professional development; improving instruction; evaluating performance; conducting action research; and demonstrating attainment of local, state, and national goals and standards. Master teachers who are candidates for the National Board for Professional Teaching Standards' (NBPTS') prestigious national teaching certificate use portfolio entries to document accomplishments of the Board's standards in their respective fields. Portfolio entries will also be used to document the accomplishments of administrators and lead teachers seeking the upcoming National Board Certification for Educational Leaders (NBCEL) sponsored by the NBPTS.

In this section, we will examine how the professional portfolio can provide you with a multidimensional representation of yourself as a professional and individual. You will discover its value in communicating to others the special talents you bring to the classroom.

Getting Started: Mentoring and Induction

When you are hired, you will likely be assigned a master teacher as a mentor who will assist you in defining your role and responsibilities. Working with a mentor to develop your professional portfolio not only supports the collaborative nature of teaching and learning; but it can also be a fulfilling and transforming experience.

If you developed a presentation portfolio during your preservice experience or for interviewing, you will want to spend time sharing it with your mentor. This will provide the mentor with background regarding your abilities and interests. Your mentor may ask what goals you would like to address as a beginning teacher. These may include goals you identified when you exited the student teaching program or those established as a substitute teacher. Perhaps your goals may be more immediate, such as learning the programs and routines of the school. Discussion around these topics will help you and your mentor establish a support program that is most beneficial to you.

You and your mentor must now determine how to organize your professional portfolio at the inservice stage. The premise of this text is that your portfolio is most effective if it is organized around a set of teaching standards or goals; thus, it is necessary to determine which standards you wish to document. Identify the professional standards that best represent your teaching level (primary, intermediate, middle, or high school), content area, or professional role. These might be different from the standards you used as a preservice teacher, and you may want to include goals set by the school and district. The standards you select will be the focal point of your documentation, so be sure that you reach agreement with your administrators about your choice of standards and the kind of evidence that you will include in your portfolio. Agreement on such important issues at the beginning of the year will ensure that your portfolio will be valued as an effective vehicle for your evaluation and advancement in the profession.

The critical perspective offered by the mentor will help you balance your own subjectivity about your teaching when compared to the goals and standards. The portfolio will continue to provide substance and focus throughout the year as you and your mentor define and redefine your strengths and areas in which you need additional support. Each of you will reflect upon experiences in and outside the classroom in an attempt to explore which curricular and extracurricular activities are best suited for you.

Your mentor can help determine ways to incorporate your experiences in the portfolio. The process of initiating your inservice portfolio produces evidence of your abilities as a beginning teacher. As you progress through your first year of teaching, you will try different techniques and strategies. This process will provide a basis for reflection. Portfolio documents such as assignments, handouts, and learner assessments help you to reflect upon the purposes you have for your lessons and the effectiveness of the daily classroom work.

Throughout the first year, the principal and other administrators will be observing you in your new role and conferencing regarding your performance. Your principal will be interested in documentation that supports what you have accomplished and how you have contributed to the school and learners. The portfolio will enable you to offer a visual depiction of your achievements through documented episodes of teaching and service to the school. It will also help you and the administrator establish an action plan for improvement and future endeavors.

By the end of the first year, you will have become more confident in your role and responsibilities as a teacher. You will have established the foundation for developing your portfolio and will be ready to begin to explore other ways to use your portfolio throughout your teaching career.

Use of the Portfolio Throughout the Teaching Career

You are now ready to explore new opportunities and avenues of learning within the school and community. Throughout your career, you can use the portfolio to assist you in taking charge of professional development opportunities and controlling the direction of your professional growth. Your portfolio, which is organized around a set of standards that you have chosen to document, will help you engage in the processes of self-reflection and self-assessment. This will guide you as you create personal goals, enhance your teaching skills, engage in action research, and make plans for your professional advancement.

REFLECTION AND TEACHER RESEARCH.   Teachers are active producers of knowledge about what works in the classroom and school. Their reflections can prompt critical questions and action research. Contributions by teacher researchers have advanced our understanding of how theory translates into practice and in turn how practice informs theory.

As a reflective practitioner, you will seek creative ways to improve your practice. The portfolio offers a useful framework as you begin to monitor, record, analyze, and document situations that prompt inquiry. The standards that you have chosen to document are guidelines for this inquiry; you can begin to answer your own questions about each of the teaching behaviors and skills that you use on a daily basis in the classroom. This process, known as action research, is one that supports improvement in instruction and facilitates collaboration with other professionals. Strategies for conducting action research include collecting data, designing and implementing plans, charting progress, collecting additional data, and analyzing results.

At times, you may find yourself involved with a partner or group of teachers working to resolve an issue or desiring to know more about yourselves as professionals. This research may begin as you and your colleagues discuss artifacts in your portfolios or share reflections about particular teaching and learning experiences. You and your partner or group may begin to observe other colleagues to further clarify an issue. Together, you will isolate the problem and seek strategies or solutions. Once again, the portfolio offers a framework for collecting and reflecting on the data. In this situation, you will share portfolio work as you search for examples of successful strategies and techniques that may be tested. Once the research is completed, the results are documented in the portfolio.

You may also consider sharing results of your research with other educators through professional journals and presentations at conferences or teacher workshops. These professional activities and the research artifacts generated through them can be included in your portfolio as demonstration of your skills as a teacher researcher. Some common artifacts associated with action research include classroom notes, literature reviews, hypotheses, sample data, rubrics, supporting evidence, and written conclusions.

Teachers who engage in action research eventually become architects of their own professional development. The cycle of action research is continual. As a teacher researcher, you will reflect upon your practice, explore what occurs in your classroom, question the use of specific teaching methods, and test theory; thus, you will begin to lay a foundation for designing your own professional development plan.

TEACHERS AS ARCHITECTS OF PROFESSIONAL DEVELOPMENT.   Who determines the content, context, and delivery of your professional growth? When you are empowered by your portfolio work, you are the best architect of your own professional development. As a teacher in the twenty-first century, you will be expected to maintain critical insight into the changing nature of your profession and to utilize strategies that will ensure your learners' successes in the future. This challenge requires you to remain abreast of current research and best practices in education. School districts typically offer ongoing education to support the professional development of teachers. In some districts, staff development is delivered to the entire faculty, regardless of specific needs. Other districts use the professional portfolio as an alternative form of professional development.

If your school district encourages you to design your own professional development plan, your portfolio is the perfect tool for doing so. There are several ways to accomplish the goal of inservice professional growth with the portfolio. One way is to use the post-observation conference. During this conference, you and your principal can determine a plan for professional growth based on the standards that are documented in your portfolio, the documented experiences that you need to add to it, and the results of your teaching evaluation. Another way to plan your inservice needs is to develop a professional development proposal based on the outcome of the action research that you have accomplished in your classroom.

Even if you do not have the flexibility to plan your own program, you can use your portfolio to aid in your professional growth. If your school district requires the entire faculty to attend all staff development programs regardless of individual needs, your portfolio is of great value to you in getting the most out of your training. Before attending an inservice training program, examine the documents under each of the standards in your portfolio and determine your needs. Ask yourself the following questions:

1. How does the training program reflect the standards in my portfolio?
2. Are there any standards in my portfolio that I have not yet documented?
3. Are there documents that indicate areas in which I need to improve?
4. What questions do I need to have answered during the training program so that I can document growth in these areas?
5. What kinds of experiences or strategies can I add to my teaching repertoire as a result of the training program? How do these experiences or strategies add to my professional growth, and how can I document them in my portfolio?

Regardless of the type of program in which you participate, you will want to continually update your portfolio to reflect your new skills and expertise. This will assist you in providing documentation for tenure, advancement, and continued employment.

Teacher Evaluation and Advancement

Portfolios are being recognized as tools for supporting teacher evaluation, rewarding outstanding practice, issuing permanent certification and license, awarding advancements, and certifying accomplished practitioners. The following are some of the benefits from using your portfolio to support these endeavors.

1. Portfolios provide a complete and valid account of what you know and can do.
2. Portfolios supply baseline documentation for ongoing assessment and teaching evaluations.
3. Portfolios offer an authentic view of learning and teaching over time.
4. Portfolios provide principals and other administrators with documentation that supports traditional evaluation forms and checklists.
5. Portfolios paint a holistic picture of the candidate seeking promotion and advancement.

Administrators who recognize the value of using portfolios for expanding the evaluation system have transformed their roles from critic or judge to that of coach and education partner. As they examine portfolios, they look for the complexities of teaching and consider the multiple assessments available. Your role is to interpret the various portable documents that support your evaluation. During a conference following an observation of your teaching or during a periodic review, you may find that the administrator will invite you to share your assessment of the performance and cite evidence to support your conclusions. He or she may ask you questions such as:

1. How can this teaching experience contribute to your professional portfolio?
2. What professional goals have you achieved?
3. What successes have you encountered in the development of your portfolio?
4. Where are you experiencing difficulty, and how may I assist?
5. How have you contributed to school and district initiatives?

Following each evaluation, you and the administrator should reflect upon the evaluation experience and establish new goals for professional growth. You should update your portfolio to reflect this recent evaluation and include new goals. Some of the common artifacts used to support evaluations include peer reviews, learner evaluations, awards, curriculum and educational resources, grants, and descriptions of contributions you have made to the school and community.

In addition to teacher performance, the portfolio has also contributed to evaluation for the purposes of preservice certification testing; approving candidates for initial certification; awarding master level certification; granting promotions, licensing, and certifications; and supporting program and curriculum evaluation. One of the most noted organizations currently using the portfolio to determine the award of certification is the NBPTS.

The Master Teacher and the Portfolio

In 1987, the NBPTS was organized to establish a voluntary advanced certification system for the nation's experienced and accomplished teachers. The Board proposed standards representing the knowledge and skills that accomplished teachers should possess based on a two-part assessment. The first part of the assessment requires that teachers assemble a portfolio of their practice. The second part requires the candidates to spend time at an assessment center where they complete a series of written exercises that probe the depth of their subject-matter knowledge as well as their understanding of how to teach those subjects to their learners.

The portfolio, referred to as the school-site portfolio, is scored as part of the assessment. Candidates are instructed to construct portfolio entries over a selected time period (approximately five months). As a candidate for National Board Certification, you are required to demonstrate evidence of good teaching practices and to document how your teaching meets the certification standards, similar to the documentation of standards that we recommend in this text. The list below shows some of the activities that you would need to undertake for the NBPTS.

1. Create and critique videos that contain key lesson components.
2. Provide detailed commentaries that conceptualize and document the effectiveness of your practice.
3. Analyze and evaluate learner responses to your teaching.
4. Provide in-depth written reflections on your teaching practices.
5. Document your development as a learner and collaborator with families and communities.

For all documents in your school-site portfolio, you will need to write goals and purposes, rationales supporting your professional judgments, and reflections.

Your Portfolio and Your Teaching Career

The portfolio as a "proving tool" and an "improving tool" is a valuable part of all phases of your teaching career. While it is a vital component of your interview when becoming a new teacher, it is much more than that. Organized around the standards that are important to your profession, it helps you to be an autonomous learner, but it also gives you an opportunity to showcase your strengths to your professors and supervisors, during your teacher education program, as well as to your potential employers. Continuing to develop your portfolio as an inservice teacher encourages your professional growth and advancement. The portfolio development process gives you a way to reflect on your own teaching practices, document your action research, support the inservice training that is required of you, prepare for recertification, and begin to experience the process required of National Board Certification. Your professional teaching portfolio helps you and others know how well you are doing. That is its full potential.

TRY THIS

1. Identifying Strengths and Weaknesses

This chapter explains how you can use the professional portfolio as an "improving tool" throughout your career. Part of your professional growth is about identifying your strengths and weaknesses as a teacher. The following exercise shows you how to do this.

1. Think of a teacher you admire and respect. What specific characteristics did this teacher have that made an impact on you? Write a paragraph that answers this question.
2. In your paragraph, highlight the specific characteristics or qualities that positively affected you as a learner.

3. List these characteristics.
4. Think about how your own personal or professional characteristics and qualities align with the characteristics on this list.
5. List everything related to teaching that you do well; call it "My Strengths."
6. List everything related to teaching that you need to improve; call it "My Weaknesses."
7. Place these informal lists in the front pocket of your portfolio notebook or in a file in your electronic portfolio. These lists can help you get started with your own professional growth, seek opportunities to meet your challenges, and focus on the strengths that define you as a teacher.

Look at the following example.

The Teacher I Admire and Respect: Ms. Acaba

I remember that Ms. Acaba was **flexible** with the topics that we learned. While teaching a unit on South America, she realized that a **hands-on experience** would help us learn more about an important industry of the countries in that continent. Thus, she arranged for us to visit a local coffee plant and tour the facility. As a native Puerto Rican and a fluent Spanish speaker, she used her **expert knowledge of the subject** to encourage us to practice the Spanish language in the classroom, even though the study of Spanish was not specifically in our curriculum. She also guided us with **authentic assignments** like a classroom newsletter and a fashion show of traditional South American dress. She created a parent volunteer schedule for adults who were able to help with these activities. I remember her as being **kind, considerate, patient**, and **nonjudgmental**. I was particularly grateful that she **did not show favoritism** in her classroom.

Ms. Acaba's Teaching Characteristics

- Flexible
- Provided hands-on experiences
- Used her expert knowledge
- Gave authentic assignments
- Kind
- Considerate
- Patient
- Nonjudgmental
- Did not show favoritism

My Strengths	**My Weaknesses**
Patient	Unorganized
Kind	Not always flexible
Easy to talk to	Need practice and confidence with math skills
Generous	
Excellent communication skills	
Believe learners learn by doing	
hands-on activities	

2. Reflecting and Sharing

In the final section of this chapter, we discuss how your portfolio can be a valuable tool throughout your professional career. We emphasize that reflection—the process by which teachers assess instruction, think critically about pedagogy, analyze subject matter, and focus on the needs and background of their learners—is a critical component of the portfolio. We demonstrate how new teachers can engage in reflection as they build their portfolio based on InTASC Standards. Teachers will continue this process throughout their professional career and build on their experiences as master teachers who are candidates for National Board Certification. In the following exercise, you will prepare a reflection on your teaching.

Select a lesson plan you have taught that includes a learner assignment. Think critically about your plan, instruction, and assessment, and then analyze your practice using the following prompts and questions.

- What worked well?
- What did each learner achieve from the instruction that preceded the assignment?
- What did each learner achieve from the assignment?
- How specific were your instructions?
- How did you analyze the learners' assignment? What did you learn from each learner's response?
- What would you do differently as a result of the learners' responses to the assignment?
- Would you give the same assignment again? If you would give the same assignment, would you change the preceding lesson or directions?
- If you would change the assignment, what would you do differently? Explain why you would make these changes.

Now, share your written reflection, the original artifact, and this list of prompts and questions with a colleague or master teacher. Discuss your reflection and share what you learned about your students and your pedagogy as a result of this teaching experience. You can also use this exercise as an entry in your portfolio. What InTASC or NBPTS standards will you select?

7

Electronic Portfolios

Technology now makes it easier than ever for prospective and practicing teachers to demonstrate teaching competence and professional growth through the use of electronic portfolios, and it is likely that you already possess the necessary skills to make that happen. Like a paper-based portfolio, the electronic portfolio that we recommend is organized around standards and contains artifacts that reflect your growth and best professional work. However, the artifact possibilities for an electronic portfolio are far more diverse. Traditional documents such as lesson and unit plans, research papers, and letters of recommendation can be complemented by artifacts such as video clips of you teaching a lesson or tutoring an individual student, an audio clip of you making a presentation to parents, or a PowerPoint presentation showing your students participating in a social studies simulation. The addition of multimedia artifacts provides the portfolio reviewer with a far richer and more complete picture of you as a growing or accomplished professional.

Creating any kind of portfolio demands a great deal of time and effort. Constructing an electronic portfolio, however, requires a different set of skills and equipment that you may not possess or have access to; therefore, the decision to develop an electronic portfolio should be undertaken after reflecting on the answers to the following questions:

1. How interested am I in an electronic portfolio?
2. Do I have the necessary technological skills (or know someone who does) to create an electronic portfolio?
3. Do I have access to the necessary equipment and software?
4. Am I willing to invest the time and effort required to develop a well-designed electronic portfolio?

If you are unsure about whether you want to undertake the development of an electronic portfolio, the information in this chapter will assist you in making that decision. If you answered these four questions in the affirmative, what follows will help get you started in the right direction. Entire texts have been written on the subject, and you will probably have to read additional material regarding the technological aspects of electronic portfolio development.

DEFINITION OF ELECTRONIC PORTFOLIOS

We define a portfolio in Chapter 1 as an organized, goal-driven documentation of your professional growth and teaching competence. It is tangible evidence of the wide range of knowledge, dispositions, and skills that you possess as a professional. An electronic portfolio serves exactly the same purpose, but artifacts are created and presented using electronic technologies, and they appear in a variety of media formats: audio, video, digital photographs, graphics, and text. Links are created to show the relationship between the artifacts and standards.

An electronic portfolio can serve as either a working or presentation portfolio. Because most artifacts are initially created in electronic form, a working portfolio can be built by storing them using a commercial software product. One method would involve storing artifacts on your hard drive in folders that correspond to the standards you are using. Be sure to back up your work using a universal serial bus (USB) flash drive or some other form of external memory device.

The purpose of a presentation portfolio is to give others an effective and easy-to-read portrait of your professional competence. An electronic portfolio can be developed using either web-based products or individual computer applications (see Figure 7.1) that will showcase your professional competence in the classroom as well as with technology. In Chapter 6, we describe a number of ways a professional portfolio can be of assistance to you as you proceed through a teacher education program, apply for a teaching position, or seek certification through the National Board of Professional Teaching Standards (NBPTS). These benefits hold true whether your portfolio is paper based or electronic. An electronic portfolio possesses unique advantages, however, due to its structure and format.

ADVANTAGES OF ELECTRONIC PORTFOLIOS

Demonstrate Technology Knowledge and Skills

A paper-based portfolio documents your teaching competence and professional growth. An electronic portfolio permits you to showcase both your best work as a professional

---

Web-Based Portfolio Programs

ePortfolio2 chalk & wire (http://chalkandwire.com/)
LiveText (http://www.livetext.com/)
iWebfolio by Nuventive (http://www.iwebfolio.com)
Foliotek (http://www.foliotek.com/)
TaskStream (https://www.taskstream.com/pub/)
ePortaro (http://www.eportaro.com/)
Blackboard (http://www.blackboard.com/)

Individual Computer Applications

HyperStudio (http://www.mackiev.com/hyperstudio/index.html)
Adobe Acrobat 10 Pro (http://www.adobe.com/Acrobat)
PowerPoint (http://office.microsoft.com/en-us/powerpoint/)
iMovie (http://apple.com/imovie)
iPhoto (http://apple.com/ilife/iphoto)

FIGURE 7.1   Web-Based and Individual Computer Applications for Portfolio Development

educator and your knowledge and skill with technology. With an electronic portfolio, it is no longer necessary to include artifacts related to the use of technology because the portfolio itself becomes documentation of your facility with computer systems and software.

Virtually every state has adopted standards describing what students should know about and be able to do with technology. As a teacher, you are responsible for ensuring that your students meet these standards. An electronic portfolio demonstrates that you possess technological knowledge and skills, thus making it more likely that you will incorporate technology into your teaching.

Facilitate Distribution

As a candidate for a teaching position, you would be understandably reluctant to leave your paper-based portfolio with an interviewer because it contains original documents that are irreplaceable. An electronic portfolio contained on a CD, a USB flash drive, or a digital video disk (DVD) is easily transportable and readily duplicated, allowing copies to be handed to reviewers at any time and in any situation.

An electronic portfolio on a CD, DVD, or flash drive can be mailed to a principal or superintendent prior to an interview or, if your portfolio is web based, you can simply include the URL, or web address, in your application cover letter. This allows reviewers to examine your portfolio prior to the scheduled interview. If given the opportunity to examine the portfolio in advance, interviewers will more likely tailor questions to the contents of your portfolio. This should work to your advantage because it focuses the interview on your documented strengths and competencies.

Store Many Documents

As we recommend in Chapter 2, a presentation portfolio should be selective and stream-lined because most reviewers do not have either the time or the interest to examine every document in your working portfolio. The structure of an electronic portfolio, however, allows you to include more than the two artifacts per standard we recommend for a paper-based presentation portfolio. Rather than manually turning pages to locate a pertinent artifact, a reviewer simply has to point and click to pull up a document or view a video. Reviewers can ignore those artifacts in which they have little interest.

Increase Accessibility

With a paper-based portfolio, a reviewer must have access to a computer to both watch a DVD of a teaching episode and a PowerPoint presentation. These types of artifacts become far more accessible when the portfolio is in electronic form and can be viewed where and when the reviewer has access to a computer: in the office, on an airplane, or in a conference room immediately before an interview.

DISADVANTAGES OF ELECTRONIC PORTFOLIOS

Time, Effort, and Cost

For some individuals, creating an electronic portfolio may require additional time, effort, and cost. You probably already possess the requisite technological and computer skills to develop an electronic portfolio. Thus, you won't need to learn any specialized skills. However, developing an electronic portfolio no doubt takes additional time and effort. Your documents have been created and stored electronically, but designing and creating your electronic portfolio requires additional steps beyond the paper-based version. Cost may also be a factor if you do not possess or have access to the software necessary to create your electronic portfolio.

Accessibility

Web-based portfolios are downloaded to a server and are there to be viewed via the Internet. By making your portfolio more accessible, however, you are creating potential security problems. Your portfolio may contain sensitive and personal information that you would prefer to remain private. You will have far less control over who sees your portfolio if you use a web-based program. To gain greater control over viewership, use a non-web-based or an individual computer application.

CREATION OF ELECTRONIC PORTFOLIOS

The steps described in Chapter 2 for assembling a professional portfolio apply as well to the development of an electronic portfolio. However, developing an electronic portfolio involves some unique considerations that you should keep in mind as you create and collect artifacts to document your competence.

Save Artifacts Electronically

Creating an electronic presentation portfolio will be much easier if you are conscientious about saving potential documents electronically. Most, if not all, of the paper-based products you create will be done on a computer. You can save a copy of the final product on your computer hard drive, but a computer crash or virus could destroy your work. A more reliable alternative is to save your work on either a CD or USB flash drive and back that up as well. As mentioned earlier, you can create folders that correspond to the standards around which you plan to organize your portfolio. You would have ten folders, for instance, if you use the InTASC standards. As you create potential documents for your portfolio, they can be placed in the folder that corresponds to the appropriate standard.

Document Your Experiences Electronically

As you proceed through your teacher education program or prepare for National Board Certification, keep in mind the unique opportunities that exist for documenting experiences electronically. Video, audio, and digital photographs can be integrated easily into an electronic portfolio, so you will want to record experiences or events that can later be included in your portfolio to document your competence or achievement of standards. This means, for example, creating video recordings of lessons you teach, audio recordings of presentations you make, and digital photographs of bulletin boards you create. While you may not use all these artifacts in your presentation portfolio, the opportunity to include them is lost unless they are recorded in the appropriate format.

Development Choices

When you are ready to actually begin the construction of your electronic portfolio, you must decide whether to use a web-based program or individual computer application software. Figure 7.1 provides a sample of web-based programs and individual software applications that you can use to construct your portfolio. In some cases you may not have a choice because many universities and colleges have purchased web-based programs for portfolio development. These programs are far more common now than just a few years ago, driven primarily by accreditation and assessment issues. Web-based programs are easy to use, and templates are provided to allow users to simply download artifacts into the appropriate locations. Users can personalize portfolios with the use of color, background designs, photos, music, and so on. One feature that makes web-based programs more desirable than individual application software is the extensive support and help system available to users. Because these programs are used by a large number of students at a particular institution, you have many people to go to for assistance and help, and formal training is almost always available.

You will need to employ an individual software application for portfolio development if you are not currently enrolled at an institution using a web-based program. You are probably familiar with many of these applications, so they will likely be easy to use. If you are not familiar with these programs, they often have extensive help and support features, and they often allow for greater creativity in portfolio development.

STAGES FOR DEVELOPING ELECTRONIC PORTFOLIOS

Creating an electronic portfolio involves two processes: portfolio development and multimedia development. The former is dealt with in detail in this book. Developing a multimedia project such as a portfolio can be described in four stages: decide, design, develop, and evaluate (DDD-E).[1]

Decide

During the initial phase of multimedia project development, you need to determine the purpose of your portfolio and the needs of your potential audience. If your portfolio will be used during a checkpoint/transition point in a teacher education program, you will need to organize your artifacts around program requirements or standards. If you are seeking a teaching position, your portfolio might be organized around state teaching standards, the InTASC standards, or standards appropriate for your particular discipline or content area. The NBPTS has specific guidelines for the organization and structure of portfolio entries to be used when seeking national certification.

You should also assess your own knowledge and skills related to technology. If you feel you lack the necessary skills to create an electronic portfolio, seek out workshops, individual tutorials, or even formal coursework. These skills can be used to both develop your electronic portfolio and integrate technology into your teaching.

If you are enrolled in a teacher education program, it is very possible your institution has adopted a web-based portfolio system, and the development of an electronic portfolio may even be mandatory. If that is the case, take advantage of the free training and workshops your department or institution offers. A somewhat less desirable short-term option would be to locate someone who possesses the necessary skills to assist you in the development process.

Design

The design phase involves determining the content of your portfolio and identifying and selecting the most appropriate software, storage, and presentation medium (e.g., computer hard drive, zip disk, USB flash drive, CD, DVD, world-wide web server). The criteria you use in selecting artifacts for your electronic portfolio are the same we recommend for a paper-based portfolio and are described in Chapter 2. The most important consideration is that the artifacts document your abilities in the professional standards you have selected. Just as with a paper-based portfolio, you want to be selective and include artifacts tailored to the teaching position or certificate you are seeking.

If you use an individual software application to construct your portfolio, an important feature is its ability to create hypertext links between your artifacts and the standards around which you have organized your portfolio. Hypertext links allow the reader to navigate effortlessly between related artifacts; this is one of the great advantages that electronic portfolios have over paper-based portfolios.

A very beneficial exercise during the design phase is to create a flowchart or series of storyboards. These are visual representations illustrating both the content of your

---

[1]Ivers, K., & Barron, A. E. (2010). *Multimedia projects in education: Designing, producing, and assessing* (4th ed.). Englewood, CO: Unlimited Libraries.

portfolio and, in the case of a flowchart, the manner in which artifacts are linked or connected in your portfolio. For instance, you might link a unit of study with a digital photograph of a bulletin board and an individual lesson plan, all placed under different standards. These kinds of design decisions are best made prior to the actual creation of your electronic portfolio.

Develop

Your artifacts have been selected and you have mapped out how they will be connected to the standards and, if appropriate, to each other. Now, it is time to begin the actual development process. During this phase, you will incorporate all your artifacts, whether they are text, digital photographs, audio, or video, into a complete program stored on a CD, DVD, USB flash drive, or some other acceptable medium.

In many cases, the experiences you documented in digital form will need some editing and/or revision prior to incorporating them into your final electronic portfolio. Video clips may need to be edited, text documents revised, or digital photographs cropped, for example. Remember that the goal, as in a paper-based portfolio, is to showcase your best work as a professional. And just like you did for a paper-based portfolio, you will want to write a rationale for each artifact in which you describe the artifact, justify its placement under a particular standard, and discuss what the artifact says about your growing competence. Rationales are a critical characteristic of any well-developed professional portfolio.

You will also want to be creative and develop an electronic portfolio that is uniquely yours. The addition of graphics, animations, or audio will make your portfolio appealing and will reflect your unique strengths and competencies. Some software programs include collections of clip art that you can incorporate into your portfolio. Numerous sites on the web offer you the chance to download and use graphics, animations, and audio files. Always read and check the permission statement and other restrictions that might apply to the individual use of these files. Permissions would also be important if you include photographs or other images of children in your portfolio.

Evaluate

During the final phase of multimedia project development, you will evaluate both the content of your portfolio and the design of the multimedia format. The artifacts should reflect your best work as a growing or accomplished professional. The relationship between the artifacts and the standard under which they have been placed should be clear. As mentioned at the beginning of this chapter, an electronic portfolio allows you to document your competence in ways not possible in a paper-based portfolio; take advantage of this opportunity.

The multimedia aspects of your electronic portfolio should also be evaluated. Is your presentation clear, concise, and visually appealing? Do the graphics, animations, and other design features enhance or detract from the overall presentation? Is it easy to navigate among standards and artifacts? Remember that those doing the viewing may have less technological competence than you; thus, the overall program should be user friendly. We suggest that you solicit friends and colleagues to evaluate your electronic portfolio and to provide you with suggestions for improvement.

http://durak.org/kathy/portfolio/
http://eportfolio.citytech.cuny.edu/esingleton/
http://eportfolio.citytech.cuny.edu/sradway/
http://my-ecoach.com/online/teacherguide3.php?projectid=4459&projectstepid=6678
http://eduportfolio.org/3160
http://oklportfolio.wordpress.com/
http://portfolio.iweb.bsu.edu/examples/stiweb/Index.html
http://sitemaker.umich.edu/lizbellus/home
http://www.departments.dsu.edu/educate/portfolioLinks.htm
http://samanthadecker.com/portfolio/

FIGURE 7.2   Websites Providing Examples of Electronic Portfolios

It is always helpful to see completed examples of any project. Figure 7.2 provides the URLs for sample electronic portfolios of both preservice and inservice teachers available for review on the Internet.

Because of the time, expertise, and resources necessary to create and develop an electronic portfolio, you may not want to make frequent changes or revisions. If you use your electronic portfolio as your presentation portfolio, you will find helpful the suggestions we provided in Chapter 6 on the use of a portfolio at the different stages of your career.

Like most challenging projects, the greatest reward and learning come not at the time of project completion, but during the development process. Creating an electronic portfolio can be a rewarding, valuable learning experience. The rewards are potentially significant, both in terms of the completed product and the skills you acquire in development. The content of your electronic portfolio speaks to your competence as a professional, while the format demonstrates your technological knowledge and skill.

TRY THIS

Developing a Flowchart

Creating a flowchart or storyboard is a necessary initial step in the successful development of an electronic portfolio. A flowchart provides a visual representation illustrating the content of your portfolio and the manner in which you intend to connect or link the artifacts.

First you need to identify the standards around which you intend to build your electronic portfolio. For each standard, begin by selecting an artifact that documents your professional growth or work. Perhaps you have developed a unit of study on westward expansion and the Oregon Trail and decided to file it under Standard Four. Begin your flowchart by placing the name of the artifact inside a box.

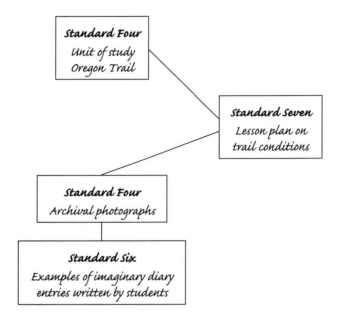

Now consider the artifacts related to your unit that would more fully document your professional competence and growth. An electronic portfolio allows you to link these artifacts to your unit of study. Complete the flowchart for this particular artifact by connecting related documents to the unit of study.

If you intend to create an electronic portfolio, the development of a flowchart is an important initial step in the planning process and should prove helpful as you begin the actual development process.

APPENDIX A

NCATE-Affiliated Professional Organizations

Many professional organizations have developed standards for teachers. Good sources of standards are the member organizations of the National Council for Accreditation of Teacher Education (NCATE). NCATE is a nonprofit, nongovernmental organization recognized by the U.S. Department of Education as the accrediting body for colleges and universities that prepare teachers and other school personnel. Over 525 institutions are accredited by NCATE. Most of the 33 professional organizations listed below have standards around which you can organize your portfolio.

Teacher Education Organizations
American Association of Colleges for Teacher Education (AACTE),
   http://www.aacte.org/
Association of Teacher Educators (ATE), http://www.ate1.org/

Teacher Organizations
American Federation of Teachers (AFT), http://www.aft.org/
National Education Association (NEA), http://www.nea.org/

State and Local Policy-Maker Organizations
Council of Chief State School Officers (CCSSO), http://www.ccsso.org/
National Association of State Boards of Education (NASBE), http://www.nasbe.org/
National School Boards Association (NSBA), http://www.nsba.org/

Specialized Professional Organizations—Subject-Specific Organizations
American Council on the Teaching of Foreign Languages (ACTFL),
   http://www.actfl.org/
American Alliance for Health, Physical Education, Recreation and Dance
   (AAHPERD), http://www.aahperd.org/
International Reading Association (IRA), http://www.reading.org/
National Council for the Social Studies (NCSS), http://www.ncss.org/
National Council of Teachers of English (NCTE), http://www.ncte.org/
National Council of Teachers of Mathematics (NCTM), http://www.nctm.org/
North American Association for Environmental Education (NAAEE),
   http://www.naaee.net/
Teachers of English to Speakers of Other Languages (TESOL), http://www.tesol.org/

Specialized Professional Organizations—Child-Centered Organizations
Association for Childhood Education International (ACEI), http://www.acei.org
Association for Middle Level Education (AMLE); formerly National Middle School
   Association (NMSA), http://www.amle.org/
Council for Exceptional Children (CEC), http://www.cec.sped.org/
National Association for the Education of Young Children (NAEYC),
   http://www.naeyc.org/

Technology Organizations

Association for Education Communications and Technology (AECT),
        http://www.aect.org/
International Society for Technology in Education (ISTE), http://www.iste.org/

Specialist Organizations

American Educational Research Association (AERA), http://www.aera.net/
American Library Association (ALA), http://www.ala.org/
National Association of School Psychologists (NASP), http://www.nasponline.org/

Administrator Organizations

American Association of School Administrators (AASA), http://www.aasa.org/
Association for Supervision and Curriculum Development (ASCD),
        http://www.ascd.org/
National Alliance of Black School Educators (NABSE), http://www.nabse.org/
National Association of Elementary School Principals (NAESP), http://www.naesp.org/
National Association of Secondary School Principals (NASSP), http://www.nassp.org/

Other

National Board for Professional Teaching Standards (NBPTS), http://www.nbpts.org/.

APPENDIX B

Developing Your "Portfolio at a Glance"

Developing a brochure will provide interviewers with a "Portfolio at a Glance" that highlights specific teaching behaviors and artifacts that reflect your professional development. With such a document, reviewers will be able to focus quickly on what you can do. This section will provide step-by-step directions for developing the brochure. Directions for this type of brochure are for the purpose of providing an example and are not meant to imply that there is only one correct way to show a portfolio at a glance.

GETTING STARTED

The development of the brochure can be divided into two procedures: writing and assembling. Steps 1 through 6 will explain how to write the brochure, and steps 7 through 9 will explain how to assemble the brochure.

Writing the Brochure

1. REFLECT on one standard at a time.
2. SELECT at least one artifact to feature within a standard.
3. FOCUS on the teaching behaviors that this one artifact shows.
4. REWORD your teaching behaviors into concise, specific statements in the past tense.
5. CLARIFY your teaching behaviors by writing directly above the name of the artifact a short descriptor of the competency demonstrated.
6. CONTINUE steps 1 through 5 for each standard.

Assembling the Brochure

1. CUT and PASTE the list of information using a larger piece of paper or a computer.
2. EDIT the contents of your draft brochure.
3. SELECT desktop-design software that will assemble your text to catch the reader's eye.

WRITING THE BROCHURE

1. REFLECT on one standard at a time. Although you will reflect on each of the standards, it will be easiest to begin with the one with which you feel most comfortable. For example, you might want to start with InTASC Standard Two, Learning Differences, which focuses on using an understanding of individual differences and diverse cultures to ensure inclusive learning environments. Use the standard as the title.

   Example   **LEARNING DIFFERENCES**

2. SELECT at least one artifact within a standard that you wish to have available at interviews. Although you may select several artifacts for a standard, these directions will focus on the selection of one. The artifact that you select should be one of which you are most proud. For example, suppose one artifact you have listed under Standard Two features writing process contracts done on an individual basis. You spent a great deal of time listening and talking with each student in order to address individual needs. You decided this is an ideal artifact to showcase in your brochure. Write a name for the artifact. For example, if you decide to use the title "Writing Process Contracts," you should write that beneath the standard.

Example   **LEARNING DIFFERENCES**
          Writing Process Contracts

3. FOCUS on the teaching behaviors that are evident in an artifact. As you read over the artifact, ask yourself questions that will help you focus on demonstrated teaching behaviors: What did I do in this lesson? How did I reach my objectives? What process did I use to reach my objectives? How were my learners engaged? What did I learn to do? By answering such questions, you begin to notice that your writing process contracts reflect several teaching behaviors. More specifically, you reached your objectives because you were able to ADAPT writing segments for English as a second language (ESL) learners, PACE content for individual success, ENHANCE clarity through the use of individual resources, and IMPLEMENT teacher modeling and peer sharing to encourage student progress. Write down these important behavioral indicators of your teaching competence.

4. REWORD your teaching behaviors as concise, specific statements in the past tense. Sometimes this may be easy because your original word choices in the rationale and artifact were especially descriptive. At other times, this may be the most difficult task in developing the brochure. Brainstorming with others or keeping a simple word list of descriptors by your side may help you select the precise word that is needed. A short word list like the following may help you get started: *adapted, administered, appraised, compiled, constructed, converted, coordinated, created, designed, developed, encouraged, engaged, enhanced, evaluated, expanded, explained, formulated, generated, implemented, integrated, interpreted, mobilized, organized, paced, planned, prioritized, produced, provided, redesigned, related, reorganized, researched, selected, sequenced, translated, utilized,* and *wrote.* Whatever verb you select, it should describe *your* demonstrated teaching behaviors. Each artifact will probably reflect more than one behavior.

Let's go back to our example. When developing the writing process contracts, your teaching involved four key behaviors. You ADAPTED writing assignments for ESL students, PACED content for individual success, ENHANCED clarity through the use of individual resources, and IMPLEMENTED teacher modeling and peer sharing to encourage student progress. Write down these statements. You now have a list of teacher behaviors that can be listed beneath the standard title, "Learning Differences," and the name of the artifact, "Writing Process Contracts," in your brochure.

Example   **LEARNING DIFFERENCES**
          Writing Process Contracts
          • Adapted writing assignment for ESL/LEP learners
          • Paced content for individual success
          • Utilized individual resources to enhance clarity
          • Implemented teacher modeling and peer sharing to encourage learner progress

5. CLARIFY your teaching behaviors by writing a short descriptor of the competency being demonstrated above the name of the artifact. Although this step may appear out of sequence, you will be able to accomplish this more easily now than you would have earlier. Look back over the list of teaching behaviors. Ask yourself one question: What did these behaviors enable me to do? In the case of the writing process contracts, you adapted, paced, enhanced, and implemented in order to show that you were "Meeting Individual Needs." Write down this statement in *-ing* form above the name of the artifact to summarize your teaching behaviors.

Example   **LEARNING DIFFERENCES**
             Meeting Individual Needs
             Writing Process Contracts
             • Adapted writing assignments for ESL/LEP learners
             • Paced content for individual success
             • Utilized individual resources to enhance clarity
             • Implemented teacher modeling and peer sharing to encourage student
               progress

6. CONTINUE steps 1 through 5 for each standard. When you finish, you will have an effective summary of your work in each standard: first, the name of the standard; second, a teaching competency descriptor; third, the name of the artifact; and fourth, a list of teaching behaviors.

ASSEMBLING THE BROCHURE

7. CUT and PASTE the list of information on a larger piece of paper. This will serve as a draft of your final brochure. Paper as large as 11" × 17" will provide the greatest flexibility as you position your information. When summarizing work in the ten InTASC standards, it works well to fold the paper twice vertically into a total of three equal sections (six equal sections counting front and back). Close the folded paper so that it opens like a book, with the left section on top. This top section will be the title page of your brochure and should contain introductory information. For example, at the top of this section, you could type "Portfolio at a Glance"; in the middle of this section, you could attach a photograph of you and your students working together; and at the bottom, you could type your name, address, phone number, and email address. The visual impact of this cover should beckon the reader to open your brochure. The remaining five sections of your brochure will accommodate the ten standards—two standards on each section (see the sample brochure on pages 102–103). As you open your brochure flat, information for each of the standards should be cut and pasted in sequential order.

8. EDIT the contents of your draft. Double-check the contents to make sure that you've guided readers to what's important. Your brochure should reflect a positive, professional image of your teaching abilities in a concise form.

9. SELECT computer software that will assemble your text to catch the reader's eye. Programs such as Microsoft Publisher, PageMaker, Microsoft Word, and Adobe Type Manager have assisted students in producing a front-to-back, three-column brochure. Whatever software you select, check to make sure that the graphic design helps to communicate effectively what you've worked so hard to produce.

PORTFOLIO AT A GLANCE

Jane A. Student

555 Any Street
Anytown, STATE 55555
(555) 555-5555
Student@anynet.com

Planning for Instruction

Standard Seven

Using Knowledge of Learners

Teaching Log

*Administered an interest survey to determine interests and attitudes of a 'reading buddy' in a third grade classroom

*Administered a running record to determine reading abilities of a third grader

*Planned twelve lessons for a 'reading buddy' based on the literacy needs and interests of the child

Using Knowledge of Curriculum Goals

Theory into Practice Project

*Held planning session with teacher to discuss objectives and goals of Medieval Times unit

*Planned a two-part lesson that taught four specific language arts objectives from the district curriculum guide

Instructional Strategies

Standard Eight

Integrating Subject Matter

Silkworm Rearing Project

*Created useful activities for many different subject areas

*Encouraged the use of related children's literature

Using Technology

Intel ProShare Collaboration

*Utilized outside resources for lesson enhancement

*Taught learners how to create WebQuests

Professional Learning and Ethical Practice

Standard Nine

Practicing Self-Reflection

Teaching Log

*Wrote self-reflective statements for twelve lessons

*Explained professional growth in twelve lessons

*Made plans for future lesson improvement

Participating in Professional Organizations

Reading Council Committee Work

*Helped start a new NCTE affiliate

*Served on the program planning committee

Leadership and Collaboration

Standard Ten

Working with Parents

Afterschool Tutoring Program

*Tutored learners at the PTO sponsored program

*Located resources and created materials for parent volunteers

*Trained parents and older adults in teaching strategies

Visiting Other Learning Environments

Community Site Visits

*Visited parent partnership programs, hospital crisis centers for children, and rehabilitation centers

*Interviewed caregivers regarding the education and well-being of learners

Learner Development
Standard One

Valuing Developmental Factors
Personal Philosophy of Education
*Described importance of understanding human development
*Illustrated the importance of matching curriculum content and strategies to developmental needs

Assessing Developmental Readiness
Case Study
*Described one learner's social, physical, cognitive, and language attainments
*Prescribed developmentally appropriate tasks to enhance this learner's development
*Implemented several developmentally appropriate tasks
*Described how the domains affected each other

Learning Differences
Standard Two

Meeting Individual Needs
Writing Process Contracts
*Adapted writing assignment for ESL/LEP learners
*Paced content for individual success
*Utilized individual resources to enhance clarity
*Implemented teacher modeling and peer sharing to encourage learner progress

Varying Teaching Strategies
Lesson Plans
*Wrote adaptation for special needs learners
*Evaluated the effectiveness of the adaptation

Learning Environments
Standard Three

Promoting Active Engagement
Card File of Poetry
*Gave incentive to use poetry
*Encouraged individual and group motivation
*Created meaningful activities to go along with different types of poems

Encouraging a Cooperative Learning Environment
Resource Unit on Seasons
*Utilized interest groups as well as heterogeneous base groups
*Encouraged the sharing of resources and information

Content Knowledge
Standard Four

Teaching History
Unit of Study on Oregon Trail
*Incorporated primary source material into unit of study
*Taught concepts in a manner consistent with how the research says history should be taught to students
*Included numerous related children's works of fiction and non-fiction

Collecting and Reporting Data
Oral History Project
*Researched history of industry in Green Valley
*Wrote interview protocol
*Conducted oral interview with selected residents of a coal patch town
*Analyzed and reported results of oral histories

Application of Content
Standard Five

Developing a Project-Based Learning Experience
School-Wide Recycling Program
*Created a school-wide recycling program
*Met district goals in environmental science and social studies
*Connected concepts and integrated goals from various disciplines

Building a Theme Study Collaboratively
Natural Disaster Theme Study
*Generated curricular concepts with teachers from multiple disciplines
*Framed content sequence based on cross -curricular connections
*Reflected with interdisciplinary team on learners' abilities to plan for a natural disaster

Assessment
Standard Six

Utilizing Informal Assessment
Moon Journal
*Provided an ongoing assessment record that monitored learner progress
*Evaluated actual learner performance

Planning a Self-Assessment Strategy
Creative Writing Project
*Enabled learners to reflect and refine their work
*Taught the writing process
*Taught learners how to set goals for writing

APPENDIX C

Glossary

artifact Tangible evidence, such as professional work samples, videos, letters, student products, or certificates, that indicates achievement of a goal or the attainment of knowledge and skills.

authentic assessment A performance assessment that measures your ability to apply understanding in authentic contexts; assignments that involve real-world problem solving or serve a meaningful purpose in a real-life situation.

Danielson's Framework for Teaching (FFT) A research-based framework grounded in the constructivist model of learning and teaching. The framework divides twenty-two components across four domains of teaching responsibility: planning and preparation (Domain 1), classroom environment (Domain 2), instruction (Domain 3), and professional responsibilities (Domain 4).

Interstate Teacher Assessment and Support Consortium (InTASC) A consortium of more than 30 states operating under the Council of Chief State School Officials that has developed model core teaching standards.

Interstate Teacher Assessment and Support Consortium (InTASC) Standards A set of expectations applicable for teachers of all disciplines and grade levels developed by the Interstate Teacher Assessment and Support Consortium (InTASC).

National Board for Professional Teaching Standards (NBPTS) An agency created to achieve two primary purposes: to develop standards in many fields for what accomplished teachers should know and be able to do and to develop a voluntary national credential for accomplished teachers that includes the presentation of portfolios based on these standards.

"Portfolio at a Glance" A brochure you create to summarize the documents in your presentation portfolio.

presentation portfolio A carefully selected, streamlined, and organized collection of work samples and other pieces of evidence that is prepared to share with others, especially with those making judgments about your achieved competence.

rationale An explanation of your reasoning for the inclusion of a portfolio artifact. It summarizes the document and experiences, explains their value for professional development, and describes implications for future work.

standards Expected learning outcomes that delineate the key aspects of professional performance. They may also be called goals, principles, performances, competencies, or propositions.

working portfolio A portfolio that is organized around standards and contains the complete collection of past work in unabridged form as well as work in progress.